Years to Remember

By

Paul M. Possemato

ISBN: 1-4033-2661-4 (e-book)
ISBN: 1-4033-2662-2 (Paperback)
ISBN: 1-4033-2663-0 (Hardcover)

Library of Congress Control Number: 2002092846

This book is printed on acid free paper.

Printed in the United States of America
Bloomington, IN

1stBooks – rev. 2/4/03

Prologue

Most of us tend to mark in time our personal history and our nation's history in relationship to other events that were occurring in our lives. An event of personal importance is related to where we were working, whose wedding we attended, what baby was born, or what song was popular. National events of importance are inter-related in the same manner. We remember where we were and what we were doing when John F. Kennedy was assassinated, when the Oklahoma bombing occurred, when the terrorists bombings of the World Trade Center and the pentagon occurred, or, for those persons a bit older, when FDR died and most certainly when Pearl Harbor was bombed. This story uses that memory bank to some degree.

Few events impacted Americans on a personal level more intensely than the years from the 1920's to 1945. In those years two historical forces came into play expanding and reinforcing the American heritage.

The depression strengthened our character through the pain and suffering it imposed. Those years forced us to face whether our democracy could survive or whether some imposing philosophy could sway us from our economic, political, and social heritage.

The war years brought us together as no other historical event has ever done. An entire society was of one mind with little to counteract both the facts and the propaganda that molded us into one unifying force. "Loose lips sink ships" carried the message clearly. Negative attitudes or opinions with an alternative point of view to impact our thinking were not tolerated. We were dedicated. Schools, churches, entertainment, newspapers and other media focused the nation as never before. Each of us had a part to play in the effort to destroy a tyranny that wanted to prevail.

"From traditions comes strength" exemplifies for me the importance of balance in our lives. Without a center, one loses focus on a core of attitudes, beliefs, and customs that help to direct sound decision-making in both one's personal and professional life. Without such a focus, there is the potential for chaos. One must know the parameters before one can stretch the limits and if necessary, with discretion, break the rules and boundaries and move toward creativity in thought and action.

My family life provided such a core. It has always been the strength that guided me.

This story tells of the impact that the years had upon me and my family as told through personal and family experiences. I recall with a fondness yet with a reality that hopefully adds to the national memory.

Chapter One

A Surprise for a Loving Son

Angelo Possemato returned to Waterbury, Connecticut following his discharge from the US Army after World War I. He had his job to come home to at the barber shop on Bank Street. His father, Luigi, lived in the Mill Plain section and Angelo, a single man, found his room waiting. He was twenty-four years old.

His friends were Italian-Americans most of whom were born in Benevento, Italy. Many, but not all, were barbers.

The barber business had not changed. The working conditions were the same as when he had enlisted. Barbers worked six days a week and from 8:00 a.m. to 6:00 p.m. Sunday was the barber's day off unless one worked a "barber boss" shop with a price cutting approach to the barbering business. The usual cost of a haircut was 25 cents with one-half going to the owner and one-half to the barber. In a 10 hour shift and if business was good, Angelo could cut 20 to 25 head of hair and thus clear about $16 to $20 per week.

Sunday was a day of relaxation for him and his friends. When weather permitted, the major activity, both before and after his tour of army duty, was playing baseball. His friends in later years said that as a left-hander, he had to be the pitcher because then as now left-handers had no sense of propriety. The pitches of left-handers traditionally curved, dropped, and sometimes were so erratic that they headed for the batter's body. Angelo also had a sweet tooth. Iced coffee, served when they played, was always sweetened with two heaping teaspoons of sugar in order to meet his taste.

Photography was still in its relative infancy. Friends felt the need to have a portrait taken in some type of a posed remembrance. One such picture was on a summer's day in a Waterbury field that served as their baseball diamond. They played in collared shirts, ties, suits, and some also wore vests. Proper attire was the correct thing to do. A photograph captured the protocol of the era. One of the players holds the bat and eight team members stare into the camera.

A few years later, he posed in a photographer's studio with two of his barber friends. Each was smartly attired with vested suit, hat, and a topcoat draped over the left arm. The picture seemed to have a purpose. As if by this photography they were reinforcing a belief that they had achieved the successful life style that was emerging as adopted Americans.

Life was good.

During his time in the US Army, both while serving at home and oversees, Angelo sent funds home to assist with his father's bills and to pay for the purchase of property in Mill Plain. Eventually he wanted to build a home there whenever he married.

On April 11, 1927, a few years after he did marry, an article was printed in the Waterbury papers. At first review, it appeared that the story was about an ungrateful son who took advantage of his father who was literate only in Italian. The story as it emerged was quite different. The newspaper story began with the headline, **"Father Claims Son Ungrateful"** and a sub heading **"Files Action for $2,500 in Effort to Recover on Property Involved"**.

The article opened with a grabber of a sentence, "One of the most spectacular cases filed in the superior court in months was recorded this morning involving an action for $2,500 damages of a father against his son. Though married, the son is a tenant in his father's house paying $15 a month rent which it is claimed his father had allowed him in order to get a "start". The manner in which it is alleged he was repaid for his generosity is the basis of the damage suit in a story of ingratitude that is rarely equaled. The action for the allegations began eleven years ago.

Knowing that the father was illiterate and could neither read nor write the English language, his son Angelo Possemato was entrusted with the purchase of three lots of land in a section of Mill Plain known as the Highlands for which the father furnished $1,640 to be paid at the rate of $15 down and $10 per month until the land was paid for. A bond for a deed was given to J.G. Twining local real estate dealer on October 23, 1916. Twining later gave a lot to the son Angelo for $340 after a down payment of $35 had been made previous to his being drafted into the army - the same terms to operate as governing three lots sold to the father Luigi Possemato.

Believing that his son would record the deed in the office of the town clerk, the father did not worry. Instead the son Angelo, defendant in the action, secured three mortgages on the three lots from Jessie A. Fogg, the Waterbury Building and Loan Association and John Stanfield, for a total of $4,900. The father asked his son for the title to the property on September 1923 intending to record it after a honeymoon. The deed to the land was put in a bureau drawer at the Passemato (sic) home to which the son had access.

He substituted a quick claim deed for the original title and when the father returned from his trip he took the supposed title and recorded it in the office of the town clerk, not knowing that it was quit claimed until some time after it had been recorded. He then asked the son for a warranty deed on the land which had been given him by Twining but the son refused it. The fair value of two of the lots today is $2,500 . The father has paid the taxes on the property as well as the principal and interest to the Waterbury Building and Loan Association .

Claims is made for a judgment to compel the son to perform the duty of his agreement regarding the land as originally stated; an injunction restraining any encumbrances during the course of the present action; title to the property; an accounting of the moneys received from the mortgages to Jesse A. Fogg, the Waterbury Building and Loan Association, John Stanfield, and $2,500 damages.

In a judgment several months later, the Waterbury papers reported **"Quick Judgment In Property Case"** and the sub heading **"Possemato Wins In Action Brought By Father"**. The article went on to report that:

After hearing a father against son law suit in superior court yesterday Judge Isaac Wolfe immediately entered judgment for the defendant Commander Angelo Possemato who was sued in a property transaction by his father Luigi Possemato.

Angelo had bought the property in Mill Plain section and when the war broke out he enlisted. The father claimed the son told him he would deed the property over to him if he continued payments in his son's absence. Papers were exchanged but were never recorded.

After the son married, the father took steps to change title to the land but the manner in which he did it was displeasing. Angelo engaged Atty. Theodore V. Meyer to defend the action. The court lost no time with the trial and in seeing that justice was done. Judgment vindicating the son was granted by Judge Wolfe a few minutes after the case had closed. It is unusual in court practice for judgments to be issued as quickly.

The evidence as it emerged was straight forward. Angelo, prior to the war, bought three pieces of property on which he made the down payment and paid the lien. When he enlisted, he told his father, Luigi, that he would send money home to pay for the loan on the property and asked that his father pay the note monthly with the money. If Angelo owed any money to his father due to unforeseen costs, he would reimburse his father when he returned from the war. The father determined that since he was the one making the payments, then he, the father, owned the property.

An article appeared in the Waterbury papers a few months after the Judge's ruling in Angelo's favor. The article was titled **"Defeats Father in Court, Then Gives Him Property"**.

The article reported that after defeating his father in a law suit, Angelo Possemato, Commander of the Wheeler-Young Post of the American Legion, is going to show he is a good sport.

Possemato was paying on property he bought on Atwood Avenue in the Mill Plain district when the World War involved the United States. He enlisted and before sailing to fight in France he told his father to keep paying on the property and that when he came back he would take care of him.

Sometime ago, when Angelo started to straighten out his financial real estate affairs, he sought to adjust matters with his father.

The elder Possemato objected claiming his son had turned over all property to him. This didn't set well with the son who had begun to take life seriously by taking unto himself a wife.

His father resorted to the courts to prove to the son that he owned the property. Angelo immediately objected and he engaged Atty. T. V. Meyer to protect his rights.

In Superior Court a few days ago, Judge Isaac Wolfe decided in the son's favor.

"Now I'm going to show that I'm a good sport," said Angelo today. "He finds he was all wrong and that I was perfectly right. Just to show him what kind of a son he has, I'm preparing a deed now. I'm going to turn the property over to him free of all encumbrance to show him that I have no hard feelings and that I love him just the same."

Copies of the court action were included in a number of articles that Angelo, my father, collected from the early 1920's well into the 1940's. The articles on politics, veteran affairs, and barber affairs, were available for his family to read, and from such articles, stories became part of family lore, and from them lessons were taught.

Chapter Two

Waterbury Politics
and the
Barber Union Movement

Dad kept a copy of the Waterbury American newspaper dated August 21, 1939 close at hand. The paper was an "extra edition" because of the news carried in banner headlines. **Hayes Gets 10-15 Years.** The second headline reported: **Leary, 10-15 years Others are sentenced. 7-12 for Carl D. Olson; Kelly 7-12 and Burns 4-8 Years at Wethersfield**. The sentences were imposed by Judge Ernest A. Inglis based upon the convictions of Mayor T. Frank Hayes and a number of city officials. They were found guilty of conspiring to cheat and defraud the city of Waterbury of more than a million dollars. In all, 23 officials were sentenced.

During the years between 1931 and 1937 Hayes deposited in an account at the Waterbury Trust Company the sum of $967,607.57 of which $207,281 was in currency. Considering that homes on large acre lots sold for $2,500 and automobiles sold for $500, the amount was indeed staggering. The convictions were a major victory for special prosecutor Hugh M. Alcorn who stated that in fact all of the details of the size of the fraud are not even known. He estimated the actual fraud at $3.5 million.

There was a lesson that was implicit in the newspaper. It was the reason that it was prominently displayed among his papers. Dad was an elected official with the Barbers' Union. He was a State commander of the Italian-American veterans. He was a American Legion officer. He chaired several statewide union and Veterans of Foreign War conventions. In all these roles, he handled large sums of money when assessed in relation to the costs of the day. The newspaper was a reminder that trust, whether public or private, is a serious matter. One who is not vigilant can be swayed even if he or she is wealthy, as was true in the case of Mayor Hayes.

A story involving financial exactness appeared in the newspapers of May 28, 1928 regarding a shortage of $106 which was income earned by a Veterans of Foreign War Post. The money was payment to the veterans for exhibiting wax statues of Ruth Snyder, Judd Gray, Gerald Chapman, and Sacco and Venzetti. Apparently the exhibitor went off with the money. The newspaper reported that Angelo Possemato, Commander, said the case of the missing money will be resolved during the coming week before things get unpleasant for the exhibitor.

In an aside as related to the wax statues, Nicola Sacco and Bartolomeo Venzetti were convicted in Dedham, Massachusetts of the killing of a shoe-master and his guard. They were executed six years later. The Sacco-Venzetti trial did not sit well with Italian-American organizations. The memory of the perceived injustice was revisited in a number of discussions throughout the 1920's and 1930's. A number of newspaper clippings regarding the case were included in my father's collection of newspaper articles of importance.

The union barber's plight in securing cooperation from barbers throughout the State of Connecticut was not an easy one.

In actuality, the struggle began right after World War I. The first fight was labeled "Bosses versus Journeymen barbers". Boss barbers kept a stable of employees who worked at a minimum wage for the owner. The boss barbers may have owned several shops or had several barbers working at one shop. The boss barbers kept prices down, basically ran a sweat shop paying a small percentage to the barbers, relied on a quick haircut, and worked on volume.

Anthony Merlino, a national barbers' union organizer, came to Waterbury as early as 1921 in an attempt to reach some consensus between the two factions. Bosses controlled the barber shops and paid a wage as they believed appropriate. Appropriate was not how the journeymen barbers saw the situation. One of the first confrontations between the barber bosses and union barbers occurred when Merlino in a speech at Forester's Hall committed national funds to begin the effort to open opposition shops to combat boss barbers. Boss barbers contended that opposition shops were an unfair type of warfare since they as the owners of shops had to pay costs of rent, salaries, utilities, and insurance.

Dad worked for Ralph Capuano's Barber Shop at 50 Bank Street - a shop he would later buy and operate. He was elected to the position of Secretary -Treasurer of the local barbers' union. In that capacity, he wrote an editorial in the Waterbury paper on September 30, 1921. In the article, he challenged the boss barbers with these words, "The boss barbers are calling for a showdown. I am positive that members of Local 732 will oblige them and send them an answer after the union's special meeting, Sunday morning at 9:30 a.m. in Garden Hall. Thank you for printing this explanation and setting our case before the public in a better light showing we are living up to our agreement in an honest way not asking for more money and not asking for less hours, but asking for justice and a chance to render an honest day's work for an honest day's pay".

The fight next went after barbers labeled "Sabbath Barbers". Connecticut had on its books a number of laws regarding prohibition of the sale of a number of merchandise items on Sundays as well as rules regarding businesses that must close on that day. Other blue laws affected general rules of conduct and business propriety. An attempt to arrest the Sabbath barbers for operating their barber shops on Sunday in opposition to the blue laws under the State of Connecticut failed. The union then tried moral and ethical approaches with newspaper editorials with titles as "Will you retire and live off the interest of funds earned by your fancy Sunday prices?"

In another effort, the union submitted to the Health Department of Waterbury a list of 33 barber shops that were claimed to be unsanitary. The union asked that the Health Department close the shops. All 33 shops were non-union and were advertising haircuts at below union levels.

This strategy was ignored by the Health Department and as Secretary of the union, Dad accused the Health Board of ignoring the petition and stated in a front page newspaper article that he wanted the rules enforced. In the article, he praised some boss barbers by name who were willing to sign an accord with the Barbers' Union. He said in part that as Secretary of the Barbers' Union for ten years, he was dismayed by the failure of city officials to enforce the law since union barbers are also taxpayers and have a right to have their concerns addressed (by the Health Department) regarding failure of some barber to operate clean and healthy shops and to use clean towels after each shave. He again attacked non-barbers for cut rate prices and opening on Sundays in violation of agreements.

In a strange twist, Dad also requested that immigration official review the number of immigrants from Italy entering the United States apparently to be added to the barber bosses stable of men willing to work for less than reasonable wages and thus undermining the unions effort to establish a living wage.

The fight then went to cut-rate price wars with some non-union barbers cutting the price of a shave and a haircut to fight the union. This price war started when the New Haven barbers joined together to raise prices for haircuts from 50 cents to 65 cents and shaves from 25 cents to 35 cents. The raise backfired and non-union barbers began to advertise their lower prices. That price war led to an effort on a national scale to unionize all barbers in the United States. President James C. Shanessy of the national barbers' union from his office in Indianapolis ordered an all out effort to achieve 100% union membership of all barbers in all cities. The Waterbury Republican reported that, at a meeting in Garden Hall in Waterbury in response to the 100% call of membership, Angelo Possemato discussing the campaign said, "One of the main objectives in this campaign will be to direct attention to improvements in the barber's standards of living brought about by the union." In the same article, Secretary Fisher of the Union was quoted as saying, "We old timers can remember when barbers worked 16 hours a day. Sunday was just another work day. Many barbers were compelled to board with their barber bosses because their income was too small to keep up more than one home. Haircuts cost 10 to 15 cents. The union has been responsible for elevating the craft standard far above these old conditions. We want young barbers to understand the value of unionism and to carry on."

In a subsequent editorial by the Waterbury American, the issue of unionism for barbers received unfair treatment in the eyes of Secretary-Treasurer Possemato. He wrote in part:

I have been interested in barber affairs for quite a few years and up to Thursday evening I believed that I knew everything that was taking place in the city on behalf of the Waterbury barbers. Now I find out that there is another and he is a reporter for the Waterbury Republican American. It is either that or he is a great story teller who has nothing to do but to pick on the poor down trodden barber in order to show that he is earning his salary. The minute a barber goes up fifteen cents for a haircut and five cents for a shave, the public declares war.

No one of the public considers whether the barber has had a raise. Yet the barber must absorb increases in rent, in utilities, and in his own rent on his home. No one figures that the barber may need an income of $40 per week to live. A customer may walk into a butcher shop and not complain of a raise of 2 or 3 cents per pound for meat but the barber who keeps a clean shop and provides a needed service with courtesy will have a customer walk out of a union shop crying blue murder.

In July, 1929, Dad took on the responsibility of developing a barbers' union newsletter titled **The Voice**. Above the masthead was the Quote "In Union There Is Strength". It was published and sponsored by Local Barbers' Union 732 of Waterbury, Connecticut. The newsletter had as its third subheading "It Pays to Look Well— Patronize Union Barber Shops".

The fight to unionize the city was carried forward in **The Voice**. The approach was to show that the barber business has changed and barber shops have become sanitary, well run establishments where men and as well women could enter with children for their haircuts. In essence, the barber shop is a far cry from the free for all establishment of rowdy men of bygone days. **The Voice** carried suggestions on running a better barber shop. It appealed to its members to circulate the publication, to continue the union fight with elected officials, to boost our friends, and to remember the enemies.

To combat the union, boss barbers decided to reduce the cost of a haircut uniformly from 50 cents to 35 cents and to cut the pay of those barbers trying to organize.

The battle for union shops continued in the 1930's. The blanket code by the President of the United States that required a forty (40) hour work week covered bootblacks, dishwashers, porters, and therefore it should cover barbers said Possemato in a statement carried in the Waterbury papers. He also reported that under an agreement of August 13, 1933, the Journeymen's Barbers' Union committed to the following:

1. No union barber will work 48 hours per week (a compromise from the 40 work week). No employee will work a barber more than 48 hours per week.
2. No operator or employee of a beauty shop can work 48 hours per week.
3. No employee or beautician can employ anyone below 16 years of age.

He also stated that a barbers' union committee will check all reported violations of these agreements.

The battle for unionization of the barber shops of Waterbury included serious vandalism. Antonio Romano's Barber Shop at 603 East Main Street was the victim of sprayed chemicals that rendered the premises unfit for work. He stated that hoodlums, saboteurs, muscle men, or what have you some time during the night of January 4, 1935 squirted large amounts of an odorous chemical through the crevice between the door jamb and the door. Mr. Romano was charging 25 cents for haircuts when the most common cost was 50 cents.

Some campaign strategies were noteworthy and heartwarming. Prior to Christmas, 1935, forty local union barbers held a free haircut day for children of jobless men of Waterbury. The event took place at Garden Hall. The barbers had advertised the event but wondered if any one would actually show. To their surprise as they arrived at the appointed time of 9:00 a.m., the line had already begun to form and before the day was over, nearly 300 children under 16 years of age, mostly boys were sheared of shaggy locks, as the newspaper report stated.

In a campaign for unionism in an atmosphere prior to union support from Washington, the barbers' union of Waterbury by and large achieved some successes. It was not a complete victory but barbers joined the union, shops closed on Sunday and Monday, and prices stabilized. However, my father's editorial comment that the public would fight every increase in a shave and a haircut came to fruition. The barber's wage which was about $100 per month or $20 per week in the early 1920's did not change markedly throughout the 1920's or 1930's and barbers in the years just before World War II were still earning at the most about $100 per month.

Paralleling his interest in barber union affairs, Dad also became active in veteran affairs. For the Italian-American, in a city run almost exclusively by Yankees and Irish, veteran affairs were a vehicle for both ethnic identity and amalgamation. Veterans who were not Italian-American were more accepting of the Italian-American veteran. Thus a mutual respect began to emerge. Dad was one of the first Italian-Americans to be elected as a Commander of a VFW group that was composed of mostly non-Italians when he took responsibility for the Wheeler-Young Post of Waterbury in January 1928 succeeding Commander Frank Downes. The newspaper articles referred to his "excellent war record" and his World War I engagements at Chateau-Thierry, St. Mihiel, and the Argonne Forest. He pledged that within a year the veterans of Waterbury would have a permanent location for their meetings.

On April 5, 1928, he organized and served as master of ceremonies at a meeting of all veteran groups of Waterbury sponsored by the Wheeler-Young Post. Veterans from the Civil War, the Spanish-American War, the American Legion, and the 304th Division [his company], were present. A special section for Gold Star Mothers was included in the convention gathering. Also present were officer representatives from Connecticut's statewide veteran organizations. The theme of the convention was better cooperation between and among all veteran organizations. William Dibble, State Commander of the Veterans of Foreign Wars spoke along with other officers hoping to brush aside any possible organization jealousies or bickering. The objective was to promote a concerted effort in securing from the United States Congress greater benefits for service men and rallying behind the accomplishment of securing approval of a veteran's hospital for the State of Connecticut.

It is of some importance to note that one week after the April 5 gathering of the veterans, Dad served as General Chair of the Dermaticians Ball on Thursday, April 12, 1928. The affair was determined by the social editors to be a social success that included dancing and only a few speeches touching upon the success of the Barbers' Union efforts.

The move to unite veteran organizations had political implications. The veterans became a solid force in political affairs. In August, 1929, veteran representatives met to organize a testimonial dinner at the Elton Hotel to honor Judge Theodore V. Meyer who had just been appointed as Judge of the City Courts. The banner in the newspaper: **Veterans to Fete Atty. Meyer, New Judge.** The subheading reported: **Possemato, Power in Soldier Circles, Chairman of Arranging Affair.**

A few days later, newspapers in Waterbury accused the organizers that the Meyer dinner was an excuse for a political rally. Possemato quoted in the newspaper denied the charge and said that politics would not be mentioned at the testimonial affair. The accusation was that the fete was a Republican rally was erroneous since, Possemato said, both Democrats and Republicans will be present to honor the Judge.

The Testimonial Dinner was held on September 9, 1929 to honor, as the program stated, Judge Theodore V. Meyer. The function was held at the Hotel Elton. The program listed Mayor Francis P. Guilfoile as the honorary chairperson with the following dignitaries present:

 Hon. Arthur F. Ellis
 Hon. Miles F.McNiff
 Hon. Harry J. Beardsley
 Hon. John F. McGrath
 Hon. Wm. J. Larkin
 Hon. Dennis J. Slavin
 Hon. E. W. Goss
 Atty. Mitchell Meyers
 Atty. Emil Hummel
 Peter M. Kennedy

Angelo Possemato chaired the organizing committee consisting of members James Di Rienzo, Charles Manganaro, Mark Margiotta, Atty. Sully I. Berman, Frank Rossi, and William Gerardi. Five attorneys were included on the reception committee: Howard Traurig, John F. Monzani, Ralph Coppeto, Michael J. Galullo, and Pasquale Di Cicco.

The file picture for the newspapers for my father had changed. From a young soldier in uniform complete with cap, the newspapers were now carrying a mature looking man of about 33 years old with mustache but now bald with only hair on the sides remaining.

Another change had also occurred in his life. Whether it was his inclination to use two to three scoops of sugar in his coffee in his youth, as his friends said, or heredity, Dad was diagnosed with a severe form of diabetes and was subject to a self-inflicted treatment throughout the remaining years of his life. The burden that he carried was a dependency on insulin injections in order to combat the diabetes.

One morning soon after he began the injection of insulin, he took the time to explain the process to his family. He had a wry sort of smile which at times almost seemed a shyness but with the grin he said that he had something to explain to us. He said that each day he would use a small enamel sauce pan that was for only one purpose. He heated water in the pan and placed in the boiling water a needle and injection tube for the purpose of sterilization. "What I am doing is to keep me healthy. I have diabetes, an illness that can be treated with a drug. I am inserting insulin into my system. Insulin was discovered by a Canadian in the 1920's as a solution for treating patients who have diabetes and can not produce insulin within their own bodies. I have to do this each morning. I insert the needle with the vial of insulin into my thigh. The injection gives me enough insulin to combat the disease for the day. Do you understand what I am doing and why I am doing it? Do you understand that this is a treatment required by a doctor?"

Watching my father inject himself daily with insulin was an expected part of life.

The concept of veteran organizations for Italian-American veterans began to come to fruition in the early 1930's. Florio Post became the center of the Italian-American Veteran's movement in Waterbury. Angelo Possemato was elected as Commander of the Post which was subsequently chartered by the State of Connecticut organization.

He chaired a number of testimonial dinners honoring V.F.W. Commanders. On Saturday, August 22, 1931 he held a banquet for M. A. O'Hara D.D.S. who was the Commander of the Department of Connecticut of the Veterans of Foreign Wars. The event was held at the Lakeside Tavern in Waterbury.

He announced a drive to gain 700 Italian-American veterans by the September 25-27, 1933 convention in Hartford. At that convention, he was elected Senior Vice Commander of the State of Connecticut.

On October 13, 1934, the first annual Columbus Day Celebration was held in the city. In recognition of the growing political power of Italian-Americans, over 130 businesses and community leaders of the city purchased advertisements in the program, including a full page advertisement by Congressman Edward M. Goss, who served as Grand Marshall. The parade began at the corner of Cooke and Grove Street and continued through North Main to West Main to Meadow and then to Grand Street, Bank Street, and concluded at Library Park.

The first annual convention of the Italian-American veterans was organized and was held in Waterbury on September 28 and 29, 1935.

He served on the general committee at a testimonial dinner of the Disabled American Veterans honoring Mrs. Isabella M. Martone on April 4, 1936 held at the Elton Hotel.

In Hartford, as the State Commander, he installed officers of the Monaco-Carlino Post No. I, on May 22, 1937. J. Vozzolo was installed as Commander and Mrs. Francis Vozzolo was installed as the Women' Auxiliary President.

At the Elk's Hall in South Norwalk, Connecticut, he installed officers at the Moscariello-Cifatte Post No. 6 on April 18, 1937. Charles Fabrizio was installed as Commander. As was occurring in so many other programs, the political power of Italian-Americans was evidenced by over 100 advertisements in the installation program.

An unusual type of program presentation occurred in New Haven of Sunday, April 25, 1937. It was a celebration honoring the Disabled Italian American veterans of the War. The entire program was printed in Italian and the ceremony was conducted in both Italian and in English. The program began with the singing of the national anthem by Soprano Miss Harriett Rebstock and Tenor Mr. David Miller and the playing of the Marcia Reale Italiana, Giovinezza, Inno Del Piave. The use of Italian in such a predominant manner was rare. Italian was spoken at meetings at our house in casual conversation, but business was conducted in English. English was the adopted language. My Mom and Dad spoke Italian when children were not supposed to hear. Those two examples were the extent of the use of the language.

In August 27-29, 1937, as State Commander, he attended the Third Annual National and State Conventions of the Italian-American Veterans held in New Britain.

On November 10, 1937, on the eve of the celebration of the Armistice, Florio Post held its annual military ball at the Buckingham Hall in Waterbury. It drew a huge crowd and was sponsored by the Italian-American veterans.

On February 12, 1938, he inducted officers at the Testimonial Banquet of the Lorenzo D'Amico Post No. 7 in Meriden.

With John D. Pastino, he traveled to dedication ceremonies in Worcester, Massachusetts; Torrington, Connecticut; Valley Forge, Pennsylvania; Trenton, New Jersey; and Boston, Massachusetts.

The Italian-American Veterans Organization was flourishing with chapters in Massachusetts, New York, Pennsylvania, and Connecticut. John De Pastino, from Waterbury, was the National Commander. A major convention of the veterans occurred in Worchester, Massachusetts on May 1 and 2, 1938. It was the largest ever turnout of Italian-American veterans who marched 3,000 strong and displayed their Post colors. Despite the prejudices that occurred as a routine part of life to Italian-Americans, life was still very good and love of country prevailed.

An embarrassing moment in the Italian-American veterans affairs occurred in September of 1938. At the parade of Italian-American veterans, a group of fifteen youngsters of Italian descent dressed in black and white Fascists outfits gave the Fascist salute as they marched by the grandstand at the Waterbury city hall. The boys and girls known as the Coro Balilla were making their first public appearance. Balilla was the Fascist organization for Italian juveniles who receive military training before becoming Italian Avanti-Guardisti (advanced guards). The leadership of the Italian-American Veterans gathered at our house and spoke of their concern because of the potential embarrassment it brought to their patriotic organization.

In addition to the salute at the parade, a German-American Bund group had purchased a large reservation of land in Southbury which was to be used as a type of encampment. My father wrote an article published in the Waterbury American newspaper expressing the point of view that there was no "German Bund" or any other type of threat strong enough to overthrow American ideals. His edited statement:

America should not fear Fascism especially if we remember the greatness of this country. Change (in America) comes not from Fascists or Bunds but directly from the people.

If there is blame for the present display of Fascist sentiment, it should be placed upon the controlled press in foreign countries who feed propaganda to America trying to impress us that Fascism will gain a stronghold in this country because of our present economic problems.

America will be defended as it has been defended in the past with patriotism that is unquestioned. That patriotism will come, in part, from veterans who are determined to keep this country away from foreign influences and entanglements. Veterans, by reason of their rights as defenders of the American principles of government, must elevate themselves to leadership especially in matters of country and flag.

On a much larger scale was the politics of the nation. At no time in our history did Congress and the President create so many laws that affected the individual existence of every American.

The politics of the 1930's and 1940's have been reviewed and rehashed by scholars and deservedly so. These years will continue to be the subject of many more books and investigations over the next century due to the significance of the players and the outcomes.

My interest is solely from the perspective of one who recalls those events from the eyes of a not quite teen-ager.

It is probably best to begin with the players themselves.

My father had a newspaper clipping of FDR visiting Waterbury. He is seated in an open air automobile. He is waving and flashing an irresistible smile with his famous cigarette holder jutting from his mouth. He exudes confidence in an age when confidence is a scarce commodity. He personifies the era. A man who overcame adversity to become the President of the United States. In this picture and in others of the era, he is aided by his oldest son, James (Jimmy) Roosevelt, who is always at his side. Jimmy Roosevelt either sits next to him or braces the President so that he can stand tall despite the fact that he can not stand by himself. He actually maneuvers in his office through the use of a wheelchair. The President's paralysis is not widely publicized because the media of the 1940's were solicitous of the interests of those in power regarding public image. FDR was viewed by the media as a leader with restricted mobility yet with absolute ability to command respect. Even at his death the press is quietly respectful that he dies with his close female friend at his side. "Mom why was there some woman with the President when he died in Warm Springs and not Mrs. Roosevelt?" "Paul, that was his secretary."

FDR chose a cabinet and advisors that seem to be blessed with names to underscore the historical moments. Cordell Hull and Edward Stettinius Jr. both served terms as Secretary of State; Henry Morgenthau Jr. served as his Secretary of the Treasury; Henry L. Stimson served as his Secretary of War; Frank Knox and Henry Forrestal had terms as Secretary of Navy; Henry Wallace served as a Secretary of Agriculture and later as Secretary of Commerce and

Labor. Alben Barkley was the United States Senate Majority Leader from 1937 to 1947. Sam Rayburn was the House of Representative Leader from 1940 to 1947.

In the Supreme Court, certain justices were prominent in the news: Harlan F. Stone, Charles E. Hughes, Benjamin Cardoza, James F. Byrnes, Hugo Black, William O. Douglas, and Felix Frankfurter. They represented an impressive line-up of judicial excellence - both individually and collectively.

All of these officials from the executive, legislative, judicial, and emerging administrative branches were regularly in the papers with quotes about national and domestic affairs. It was an age of giants of men with memorable names and big jobs or an age of remarkable moments that made giants out of ordinary men through the jobs that they held.

Franklin Delano Roosevelt also seemed to know how to rally the troops. After the bombing of Pearl Harbor occurred, he made it clear that Japanese diplomats were in Washington talking reconciliation with the United States. His words made it clear that the Japanese attacked Pearl Harbor while lulling us into believing they had good intentions. The Saturday newsreel showed the Japanese envoys leaving the White House following a conference just days before the surprise attack. Such drama played well to enrage the nation against the enemy. Years later, many scholars have proposed that the United States had broken the Japanese codes and knew that the attack on Pearl was imminent.

FDR was also determined to stay in office even though he was ill. As one read the papers, it seemed clear that he made an agreement to remove his 1941-45 vice-president from the ticket and substitute a party faithful - Harry S. Truman. Newspaper and radio commentators seemed reluctant to debate the issue. Was Henry Wallace a dangerous liability because of his liberal sentiments? Newspapers true to the image agreements of the 1940's rather talked about the need for Wallace in key position and thus the change. It was a political expediency that had to be learned if one were an avid reader of the politics within the daily newspaper.

The 1940's election also raised into the prominence the concept of "One World" as proposed by the Republican candidate for President, Wendell Wilkie.

Politics was not just in Washington. Douglas MacArthur was both a liability and a blessing. It was clear from veiled commentary that he was feared by the ins of Washington even though he was admired by the public. MacArthur's ego, however, was evident in the manner in which he left the Philippines within a famous quote of, "I shall return." His manner which seemed to demonstrate an unusually high opinion of himself presented an enigma to the boys of my age. On one hand, he was a leader in that he could instill dedication and commitment in his troops much like George Patton. On the other hand, he appeared to be smug and overbearing to me and to others my age. The well controlled press of the war years did not spell out as clearly that there was a debate occurring over who was in charge of the military strategy of the Pacific campaign. Between the lines, one read that a debate was indeed occurring among super egos. MacArthur's insistence that the Congress and the military decision makers in Washington fund his return to the Philippines by a land assault was repeatedly rejected in favor of a victory by sea. Eventually some funds and supplies came to him and he was able to win a land victory in concert with the destruction of the Japanese navy by the United States fleet. Yet he was clearly a force to be reckoned with in the politics of the future and newspaper accounts talked of a possible run eventually for the Presidency.

The politics of the 1940's was a learning experience that demonstrated by example that even the most highly regarded may have weaknesses of character. I compared a number of these men to my own heroes who seemed to go about their tasks with a quiet but resolute intention to do their best. My mother and father who faced such adversity through depression and setbacks were my heroes. They instilled an ethic in all of their children that one who brags or displays the need to tell how good he or she is may be lacking in fundamental virtues. Teachers were also among my greatest heroes. I admired them for their dedication and their determination to have all children achieve. I especially appreciated that they were diligent in ensuring that I conformed and responded to their motivation. I also placed at a high level the quiet manner that Joe DiMaggio went about his role. He seemed so capable and so willing to let his ability speak for itself. He did not need to tell us how good he was. It was a lesson to be learned and practiced by me for all my life.

These lessons at first might seem to be beyond the level of a sixth grader, and it is not my intent to overstate my understanding. However, politics had became a love and an obsession. It was clear to me that as the war neared its close each day seemed to play out the basis of stepping stones for the heroes of the war as they viewed their future. The 1940's were great learning years because they presented drama on an immense screen. The politics was not only the politics of the nation but the emerging politics to influence the world.

Chapter Three

Mill Plain

In the early 1930's very few families had money set aside for hospital expenses so being born at home was a high probability for depression babies. And so that is where I was born, at home. Home was 335 Atwood Avenue, Mill Plain, as it is called, in Waterbury, Connecticut on September 29, 1933. My mother and father named me after my mother's father, Paul, my first name, and Michael, my middle name, because September 29th is the feast of St. Michael the Archangel.

My mother was Albina Mocciola (sometimes written as Mocciolo) Possemato, Her mother and father were Theresa De Joseph Mocciola and Paul Mocciola. My grandmother, Theresa, was born in 1877 in Anzi, Province of Potenza, Italy to Angeline De Stephan De Joseph and Rocco De Joseph. Paul was born in 1871 also in Anzi, Potenza, Italy to Maria Guiseppe Cassella Mocciola and Rafaele Mocciola. The De Joseph's and the Mocciola's were city people who had trades and had some means of a livelihood. Among the ancestors were shopkeepers, makers of shoes, priests, and an archbishop of Basilicata. My mother's great grandmother on her mother's side was Spanish. My mother's great grandmother on her father's side was French. Paul's two brothers and two sisters all attended and graduated from school. Paul refused to attend and became a problem to his father, Rafaele. He was sent to France for eleven years to live with his grandmother. When he returned from France, he was apprenticed to a shoemaker and in time became a skilled craftsman. At age 23, he met Theresa, age 17, and in November, 1894, they were married. In the spring of 1895, they came to the United States on their honeymoon. They sought legal entry as immigrants and thus became part of the early migration of Italians to the United States. They moved from one large city to another including Jersey City, Philadelphia, where they lived in a tenement across from where the Liberty Bell was housed, and New York. Eventually they moved to Waterbury, Connecticut.

My mother was born in Jersey City, New Jersey on September 14, 1901 and was named after the Polish mid-wife who delivered her. Her mother told her that when she was born, the newsboys were pedaling a special addition newspaper that President McKinley who had been shot died of his wound.

My mother had four sisters, Mary, who was four years older than my mother, and four younger sisters, Helen, Eva, Mildred, and

Angela, who died as an infant. She also had two brothers, Ralph, who was the oldest child, and Adam. Adam died at eighteen of influenza in 1926. Ralph served in the US Army during the Mexico border campaigns. After discharge from the Army, he joined the Marines (never, he said, say U. S. Marines because there is only one Marine Corps in the world). In W.W.I, he was gassed, never had a good stomach, but lived to be 95 years old.

Grandpa Paul was the owner of a custom made shoe and boot shop for many years in Philadelphia and New York. Later, as he grew older and as shoemaking became difficult for his hands, he worked for the US Time Corporation in Waterbury.

My paternal grandfather was a farmer from the town of Vitulano, Benevento, Italy, who in 1904 at the age of 33 decided to leave his family and come to America with the intent of sending for them when he had earned enough for their passage. His family consisted of his wife, Maria Michela Tartaglia Possemato, my father, Angelo, the oldest and at the time nine years old, his sister, Mary, seven, and a third sister Philomina, five years old. When my grandfather arrived in the United States, he obtained work as a machinist at Scovill's in Waterbury in order to save money for the family's eventual trip to the United States. Before he could raise the funds, a decisive event occurred according to family lore. My grandmother, now working for her brother-in-law in the fields in Italy for the three years that her husband was gone, was told one day that she was not working hard enough and was struck with a stick by her brother -in-law. With that, she got up from the ground gathered up my father now 12 years old and his sisters and off she went to America in 1907 using whatever money she could raise from the sale of her possessions, leaving behind the land which belonged to her husband.

My earliest recollections of my paternal grandfather is that he grew vegetables: tomatoes, herbs, green beans, peppers, and squash to name a few. I also remember that he never talked to his grandchildren even though we lived next door with only a vacant lot between us. On an occasion he would gesture to us to pick a tomato and eat it. Or on other occasions, when he killed a pig, he would give us a piece of pig's blood pie to eat. That was basically it. No sitting at grandpa's knee, no friendly hugs, and no smiles of love and affection.

It may also have been that for many years Grandpa Possemato was a lonely man for all things did not work out so well after my grandmother arrived from Italy. She bore him three more children two boys and a girl. When the third boy arrived, and as happened so often in those days, Grandma died. Grandpa was left with raising several of the children alone. My father, who was nineteen when his mother died, had already been working for seven years as a barber's apprentice and then later as a fully licensed barber and thus was not a problem. The two older girls married young. That left a nine year old, Dominic, a four year old, Anna, and a baby, Albert, to raise. So some of his coldness and bitterness might be forgiven.

My father Angelo and mother Albina were married in 1923 at Immaculate Conception Church across from the green in Waterbury. Mom, as evidenced by her wedding pictures, was a beautiful woman. Her friends, when she was young, called her "Theda" after Theda Bera because she looked like the "vamp". Our family consisted of my sister Michelina (Lena) - 1924, my brother Louis (Lou) - 1926, my sister Theresa (Tessie) - 1929, my brother Angelo (Junior) - 1931, and me (Paul) - 1933.

Children arrived every two years except in 1928. In 1928, a boy was still born - thus the gap. When each of his children were born, my father made a home-made Italian liqueur, labeled it for the baby and put on the label "not to be opened until 21 years of age". On my bottle - strega - he put "full house three king and two queens". In reading the label when growing up, I believed that I would never had been born if the baby between Lou and Tessie lived. My father would have had his full house after Angelo Jr. and that would have ended it. So taking a positive attitude, I believed that I had a destiny to fulfill. Over the years I barely missed being done in on two occasions, so thus I decided that this destiny was in fact a reality.

With financing available for home construction, my parents, in 1929, built the Mill Plain house on about two acres of land. The downstairs had a kitchen, dining room, den, parlor, separate entry, and a smaller bath. A center staircase at its base made it possible to turn right into the kitchen or left into the parlor. Heading upstairs, by way of the staircase, there were four bedrooms and a full bathroom. The house was built with a full cellar. The cellar, accessible from kitchen stairs or the outside cellar door, included storage areas, canning shelves, the heater, the coal bin, and an area where spiced meats and cheeses were hung from rafters for curing. On the east side of the house was a verandah which ran the length of the house and overlooked a lot between our house and Grandpa Possemato's house. In that lot was the garden. On the west side, was a vacant lot also owned by my Mom and Dad. The lot lay between our house and the Maroni's house. The Maroni's were my Dad's sister Mary and her husband Jim.

The west side of the house had a side entrance from the kitchen and on those steps when I was three years old sister Tessie taught me to tie my shoes.

It was on both the west and the rear side of the house that the parties were held. A fire pit was permanently built for use as a warmer on cool evenings and a place as well to roast marshmallows and cook hot dogs. It was that pit into which I was pushed with regularity by my cousin Richard. Richard was one year younger and the only child of my Uncle Dominic and Aunt Julia. "Mom, he did it again.", was my complaint. "Don't worry, you aren't hurt and besides he is younger than you.", was the response.

Mill Plain in the 1930's was rural for a city the size of Waterbury. Not rural in the sense of farms and barns but rural as in undeveloped. My recollection of a road crew coming through and paving the dirt street is vivid. It was a hot day in the late 1930's and my mother made a pitcher of lemonade and said, "Paulie take this pitcher and these cups to the workers". They were sweating and mopping their brow. Atwood Avenue, however, had a paved road.

My mother's concern for those people less fortunate and in need was generous but tempered by a certain puritanical righteousness. She would help those in need if they were willing to work. She would give English language lessons for her Mill Plain Italian neighbors who wanted to learn the language. She would not charge for the lessons, but those persons who took lessons had to study and come prepared the following week.

She was greatly concerned for men out of work during these depression years. She would tell us that men out of work were not to blame. Times were difficult. "We have a roof over our head." It was one of her favorite expressions. The reports of vagrants in Waterbury living in shacks at the golf lots off Thomaston Avenue brought tears to her eyes. "At least the Brookside Home opens their doors when it is cold to let them spend the night."

Growing up the youngest in Mill Plain was not an easy task - partly because the youngest is spoiled and at times also can be obnoxious. But in fairness, I am the product of all kinds of fears and superstitions that were thrust upon me in response to my poor behavior and ego-centric attitude. Looking back, it seems that I can identify most of my anxieties and fears and as well the root cause for most of them.

My brothers and sisters drove me into what one could now call "anxiety behavior". As the youngest, I was a problem to be sure. So to torture me they would instill major fears such as a dread of the rag man. The rag man drove a cart pulled by a horse. On the cart he had rags that he sold or purchased from his customers. Rags for sale! Rags for sale! I would run and hide because if I were not good, my brothers and sisters told me, they would give me to him. Strangers, who in the 1930's would often knock on the door to sell or ask for food, were also an impetus to raise fears in me by my sibling. If I were not good, they would give me up to the peddler or the hobo -never would I be seen again. When the door knock came or even when guests would come into the house, I would head under the nearest furniture. There I was safe. Of course, my mother and father viewed my behavior as "he's very shy". It wasn't shyness; it was survival.

One vivid memory is of Judge Theodore V. Meyer. He was born in Tennessee, attended Cornell Law School, graduated in 1913, and eventually settled in Waterbury. He enlisted in the US Army in World War I and was commissioned as a lieutenant during the war. My father served as an enlisted man under him. Some time after the war, Judge Meyer was selected and served as a Judge on the City Court of Waterbury. He was, as I recall, an extremely handsome man. He had white hair, a mustache, and was always well-dressed. He parted his hair in the middle or very close to it. Judge Meyer was about three years older than my father. My father had also volunteered to serve in the US Army during W.W.I The Judge and my Dad maintained a reasonably close relationship given the difference in the status of the two - as defined by 1920's-1930's standards. Judge Meyer would visit to discuss veteran affairs since he was also a Commander of an American Legion Post as was my father. When he arrived, I would head for a safe place under the furniture. The Judge also smoked cigarettes something I had never seen before. I remember on only one occasion my father smoked a cigarette even though he always smoked a pipe.

As the years went by, I asked my mother what had happened to the Judge because at a certain point in time he did not visit any longer. She told me that he began to drink. It was sad to look at a picture the family had of him to think that he seemed "to drop out of sight" because "he drank". Years later, he surfaced again, became re-established, and was a founder of the Boys' Village in Milford.

A few of the peddlers were tolerable - especially the cheese man. He had the accent of an Italian immigrant . He would call out "ricotta fresco" which sounded when he said it like "ricottafraish". His wagon smelled good and woman would come out and buy. He would not invoke the run and hide syndrome in me. Rather, his presence was one of food that smelled good and was my earliest recollection of things Italian.

It was not difficult to understand that I feared dogs even though we had a dog. Well "had" is a bit out of context. My father owned a dog that was the perfect watch dog. He was always tied to a post in the ground, and he was mean. His Italian name was "Conte" which means "Count" in English. He was an Italian pit bull dog and frankly had to be chained because he, like all pit bulldogs, had a mean disposition and jaws that, we were told, would lock on when they bit. "Conte" eventually had to go. Only my father could get near him.

With my brother's Lou's urging, Dad brought home another dog. This one was gentle and well-behaved. He was an Alaskan Spitz, named Beauty, with a heavy and pure white coat. He was allowed to roam the yards between our house and my Grandpa's. He was with us for about a year. One morning, Dad found him dead. Apparently he had eaten the poison used by my Grandfather as a spray to protect his grapevine. The loss of this gentle dog was a blow to the family. We never again had a family dog.

I should have had a fear of my brother Junior but I did not. We were thrown together for the first fifteen years of my life. We had to share a twin bed together all those years. We always "ran" together through the early years. Junior, however, was different. First, he was stronger than anyone his age or for that matter those older as well.

Family lore says that the doctor upon delivering him said that he had the biggest shoulders of any baby he had ever delivered. Junior, when he was young, had a temper. On one occasion when he was angry, Junior picked up the five gallon oil bottle that fed the oil stove and turned it upside down to empty it. The bottle was a bit smaller than the size of today's water bottles that are delivered on the shoulders of a Sparklett's or Arrowhead man. He would throw things: books, scissors, whatever, and usually at me. If Junior was upset with Mom, he would head for the living room and turn over the furniture. The furniture was bigger than he was. My father had difficulty to say the least in disciplining him. Nothing really worked until he actually grew out of it at the age of eight or nine. But those times were thrilling for a younger brother who was often the target of his anger. A curious thing though as a final note on Junior's early exploits. His aunts and neighbors who knew of his rampages would marvel at his behavior once outside the home. "Oh, he is a devil at home, but Junior is a saint when he is in school or at his cousins etc."

On my sixth birthday, my father in a playful mood began to "spank me" six times and one to grow on. Typical of my "fearful of everything" state, I, on my birthday, began to cry-much to his confusion.

There are many memories of Mill Plain through the years up to 1939. Some are a bit painful, and some are pleasant and long lasting. My grandfather. as an example, had a Caruso collection on the old cylinders. One day, my brother Lou decided to play baseball with the disks because they were no longer wanted and that is the way some great recordings served as baseball fodder. The story is still told today usually when recounting with humor how much treasure is earned when others sell collections of whatever and we calculate how much the family lost through smashing out make-believe singles and doubles with those Caruso cylinders.

Lou and Dad had a special bond. As the oldest boy, he was raised when Dad was still younger and playing sports. So it was not unusual for them to enter various tournaments or to play ball together. As an example, in the early days of Mill Plain, father and son horse shoe tournaments were held. Lou and Dad each year seemed to capture the first place prize.

There are other pleasant memories. There was always a feeling of safety in that home. No matter what the conditions, the family was secure. I recall on many occasions looking out the kitchen waiting for my older brothers and sisters to come home from school and feeling a sense of peace and wellness as I stared without concern at the Atwood Avenue road. That feeling of tranquillity is best described as a feeling of peacefulness in my stomach. Such a sense has always been with me when considering my degree of well-being.

One could pick blueberries along the empty lots on Clearview Avenue and have them with milk for breakfast. And then there was Sandy Bottom - a favorite swimming hole of the 1930's. Walking to the end of Atwood Avenue turning right on Clearview to Mansfield Avenue and then heading down a dirt road would get us to the swimming hole. It was actually a pond whose water was dirty brown but a spot to have fun on any summer day. It was at Sandy Bottom that I learned to swim. First under water and then a primitive stroke that kept me afloat. Sandy Bottom is also where Junior gained a fear of the water which exists to this day. His introduction to swimming is not recommended. Oldest brother Lou decided to teach Junior to swim by throwing him into the water from a small dike just to the right of the beach. The result was a floundering near drowning seven year old who would never go near water again. (Today Sandy Bottom has been replaced by the Naugatuck Shopping Center. Oh Well!)

Mill Plain was a place where family gathered. Often it was my mother's mother and my mother's sisters and their families. On any Sunday, Grandma Mocciola, aunts, and cousins would walk from the middle of Waterbury to Mill Plain to spend the day. Sometimes it was Grandma Theresa and Aunt Mary Capella with her five children - Nick, Paul, Lucian, Joseph, and Grace. Another time it would be Uncle Ralph with his daughters Theresa and Josephine. Josephine died of a ruptured appendix in 1937. Aunt Helen would come with daughter Beth. Aunt Eva who would not marry until 1945 was a frequent visitor and a close friend of my mother. I do not believe that Grandpa Mocciola ever visited Mill Plain.

Christmas in Mill Plain was not the celebration that one might typically associate with the holiday. My remembrance is that as a young child, we did not have a tree or presents. Frankly, they were not missed having never experienced them. The family attended mass at St. Peter and Paul, as we did every Sunday, and then gathered in the early afternoon for a Christmas meal. My father, whether there was money or not for many other needs, always made sure that his family had food on the table. We may have had shoes with cardboard to cover the hole but feeding the family was a priority. Christmas like Easter and Thanksgiving was a day for a feast. A typical meal was lasagna; bracciola involtino (a meat stuffed roll); melanzana parmigiano (eggplant layered with cheese and battered with eggs); and Italian salad, always eaten at the end of the meal and before the dessert. My mother was a good baker of pies but not cakes. In fact she made the best burnt cakes that I have ever tasted. But her pies were wonders - especially the ricotta pie, an Italian cheese cake pie, or her fruit pie which was made with a condensed milk batter.

I loved to watch my mother or my father cook. There is an art to cooking and a flair if one is so inclined to be creative. Bracciola is an item that is worth the watch when it is being made. Starting with a lean flank steak, usually pounded for thinness, which is then laid flat for stuffing. The stuffing consists of olive oil to moisten the meat and then layers of bread crumbs, salami, provolone, coppicola, and hard boiled eggs. The meat is rolled and tied with string and then baked. My father also made the fattest and juiciest meatballs. His secret was to include a minestrone soup as one of the ingredients.

It was a fall day in 1937, that, as a four year old, I saw my first airplane. During those days, I was the last one at home and not attending school. I would be with my mother on her once or twice a week visits to the neighbors or her sisters-in law, Mary Marrone or Julia Possemato. On one occasion at the home of a neighbor, Mrs. Sistilli, we heard an engine noise and ran out to look at a two-winged airplane that Mrs. Sistilli said was a US Mail plane on its run. It had probably strayed over the Mill Plain area she said. It was a site never to be forgotten. To this day, I can remember looking up and seeing that plane, with its US insignia, and the pilot who waved at us.

To understand my background a little better, it may be best to relate my father's background. He was born on October 4, 1895 in the city of Vitulano, Benevento. He was baptized at San Pietro Apostolo Parish in that city.

Upon arrival in the United States, he went to school for about two weeks in the second grade and never went back. He once said that he walked in the front door and out the back. Over the years, he became literate in English without trace of an accent mostly by reading. In our home were the Harvard Classics, the complete works of A. Conan Doyle, Booth Tarkington, Kathleen Norris, the Book League of America including Shakespeare's complete works, Ibsen, Emerson, Ely Culbertson, Defoe, Oscar Wilde, and Tolstoy. He also had a collection of books on detective stories. He continued to speak and write Italian as organizations and responsibilities in those organizations may have demanded. After his two week stint at school, he began working as a barber's apprentice. Typically, in those days, an apprentice would begin by sweeping floors, then shaving, then trimming, and then actually giving the customers a haircut.

At twenty-one on September 17, 1917, he enlisted in the United States Army at 110 Bank Street, Waterbury. He applied and was granted US Citizenship on June 25, 1918 at Camp Devens, US Army Base, Ayer, Massachusetts under special provisions for US Army enlisted men.

In July, 1918, his father received a postcard, government issued, from the American Expeditionary Forces. It read, "THE SHIP ON WHICH I SAILED HAS ARRIVED SAFELY OVERSEAS".

Name: (hand signed) Corp. Possamato
Organization Company 304 Inf.
American Expeditionary Forces

Below the signature (spelled Possamato) was a handwritten note that read, "All is well. Will write letter soon."

He served in France with the American Expeditionary Forces beginning July 8, 1918. He obtained the rank of corporal, saw combat from July to November of 1918, received an honorable discharge (honest and faithful in his service) on June 30, 1919, and received a Bronze Victory Button.

My father was willing to volunteer and throughout his adult life he was a joiner who took responsibility. In 1931 and 1932, he served as Scoutmaster for Troop 26 of Waterbury. Dad was also patriotic. He demonstrated that feeling more than he talked about it. He belonged to several organizations including: the American Legion - Corporal Coyle Post Number 1, the Veterans of Foreign Wars - Wheeler-

Young Post Number 201; and the Italian-American Veterans - Florio Post - named for Bugler Nicholas Florio killed in combat in W.W.I at Chateau Thierry - the first Italian -American to die in the War. My father honored the soldiers who died in the first World War. He would remind us that brave men had died for this country. Thus, in addition to Florio, we knew the names of other Waterbury boys killed in action in WW I- Frank (Jake) Coyle, Lt. Patrick F. Shea, George Franklin Wheeler, and Gilbert A. Young - to recall a few.

My mother belonged to the woman's auxiliary of the American Legion and Veterans of Foreign Wars organizations. Like my father, she usually served as an officer in the organizations. It is also typical of Italians that when one family member belongs, several follow suit. Thus the women's auxiliary, which had as its President Albina Possemato, also had as members of the organization, Mary Cappella and Mildred Pazerras (sometimes spelled Pazeras), her sisters.

My mother was very proud of her election as President of the Auxiliary on October 22, 1938. Within her was a bit of the public speaker and the politician. She was especially pleased by the cards and notes of congratulations she received. Over the next few weeks she would read them to us. They included:

- Canadian Legion Auxiliary #94 Rhea Laurence - President
- David L Farmick Auxiliary #91 Post of the Jewish World War Veterans of the United States - Mollie A. Fidler - President
- Lieutenant Shea Auxiliary VFW
- Guiseppe Insane Auxiliary
- Frank Mendillo Post #5 New Haven
- Ladies Auxiliary Nicola Bernadino Post #2
- Y.D. Auxiliary - Mrs. Florence Shaeffer President

Our Mill Plain home in the 1930's was the "getting ready point" for patriotic parades. On Memorial Day and the Fourth of July there were wonderful parades with fife and drum corps that New England has in abundance and which the eastern states seem to generate so magnificently. Lou played the fife in the Waterbury Fife and Drum Corp. Lena dressed in costume was a majorette type. Uniforms in the style of the Revolutionary War were typical dress in the parade as were the uniforms of the Spanish-American and World War I worn by those veterans. Following the parade a dedication usually occurred at Library Park where an honor roll of Waterbury veterans who died was called with a benediction spoken usually by Reverend Roger T. Anderson or Reverend J. Oliver Cronan. The benediction was followed by a moment of silence. After the memorial, the house on Atwood Avenue would be filled with friends from the Legion and VFW. Friends remembered included Michael and Edith Giordano, Eustachio and Louise Schiappa, and John and Rose Candido.

John Candido was one of my father's closest friends. He, like so many Italian barbers born in the Benevento region of Italy and now here in America, was part of a group that remained together. They had the same language, the same culture, and the same hopes for a better life. John was also a musician, and as a young man, he played in the Waterbury Boys' Club Band. The band had several Italians as members including Henry Muccini, Joseph Muccino, Jerry DiPietro, William De Vincent, Vincent Ippolito, Earl Rossi, and Angelo Jacovino. The band was led by George Gentile. But there was little money in being a musician so John became a barber. He bought a house on Atwood Avenue, down the street from our house and generally my Dad and Mom and John and his wife Rose shared most life's major moments together in the days before 1945.

Michael Giordano and his wife Edith were also visitors to the Mill Plain home. Michael Giordano was a veteran of the World War and was a holder of the Purple Heart. He served in the 102nd Infantry of the Yankee Division and was gassed at Chateau Thierry. He was active in veteran affairs with my father as a member of the Florio Post and the Cpl. Coyle Post of the American Legion. He was born in Italy and came to Waterbury in 1905 as a 14 year old. He, however, was not a barber, working as a maintenance staff member at Wilby High School.

Domenic Del Donna was about ten years older than my father. He was also born in Benevento, Italy. He came to the United States and Waterbury in 1898 and owned a barber shop. My vivid memory of Domenic Del Donna is his thick white hair.

During these gatherings the typical conversations tended to settle mainly on three or four favorite topics.

On a few occasions, stories of the days in France with the infantry was a favorite with remembrances on the places in which fighting took place and subsequently on places visited after the war was over and before the doughboys were shipped home. On one occasion, I recall my father talking about his visit to Biarritz in May 1919. He had been inside the Casino Bellevue, spent time on the beach (Le Grande Plage), walked the Holy Virgin Bridge, walked on the Rock of the Basta, and went inside the Regina Hotel. For a twenty-three year old, it was an experience that he never forgot. Jokingly, he would use a few words and phrases in French from time to time. I am not sure but one seemed to have a certain risqué flavor.

A second topic was the barber business. The objectives of the barbers was to create a barbers' union and to settle on two days that barber shops could close (Sunday and Monday) with full cooperation of all barbers so that no cut-throating would occur, and the desire to see some stabilization of barber prices throughout Waterbury.

A third topic was the history of Benevento and the importance of the province in the history of Italy. These Beneventons agreed that Benevento was "the other Campania" with no ties to Naples and the Gulf of Naples. The people from Benevento were descendants of Samnites, a proud race who fought with the Romans for the glory of Rome and Italy. The talk conceded that the Benevento state was captured by the Longobords around the 6th Century and most of the people of Benevento trace their ancestors to the Longobords.

A fourth topic was always baseball and discussion centered on which was the best team in the major leagues. In the 1920's and 1930's, as the conversation went, the team of preference was the New York Giants; however, as Crosetti, Lazzeri, and DiMaggio began to capture the sports' spotlight, more and more Italians of all ages began to drift toward the New York Yankees.

The meal at these Mill Plain gatherings might be pizza (pronounced apizz) on an occasion purchased at Savan Rock but usually purchased at a favorite Waterbury pizzeria. On some occasions, hot dogs and root beer were served and always watermelon and cherries. Ice cream cake packed in "dry ice" was a usual dessert. It was a time of simple pleasures and great love of country.

Money was not discussed around the five children. As time went on, it became apparent that money, or the lack thereof, would be a factor in our life. But for the moment on those middle and late 1930's, money was not yet such a determining issue.

My brothers, sisters, and I understand that some people had money and were comfortable because of it. Mr. and Mrs. Morton were a very stately couple who would drive down Atwood Avenue in a clean and shiny automobile of 1935 vintage. It was green and black and beautiful. An automobile was a rarity. When my mother would tell us that Mr. and Mrs. Morton were driving by if we wanted to see the car, she would often say that they had lots of money to buy things. I asked, "Mama, do Mr. and Mrs. Morton own Morton Salt?" "No, but they have lots of money".

Some people living today may remember the blizzard of 1938. It snowed for days and the results were drifts of snow that piled eight to ten feet. On one such day, as it snowed unrelenting, my mother waited by the door for my father to show himself over the hill. He was late and she, who was always a worrier, worried more than ever. Mother made worrying a family affair. My father would take the bus from East Main to Meriden Road to Academy Road and then to the bottom of the hill at Atwood Avenue. The route with transfers was time consuming but on this day with the heavy snow, the time taken for the trip was unusually long. He managed the bundles in each arm as he trudged along. He shifted packages for distribution of the weight and hoped to be home with each step.

As Mom began to worry more and more and as the minutes then hours passed, she told us of other blizzards that had descended on Waterbury. "March is a bad month. You think we are out of the snow and then it hits us. We had a terrible snow storm when I was a young girl just before the World War, in about March 1916. It seemed like the snow would never stop. It snowed for about 11 or 12 days straight." She talked to no one in particular but continued to watch out the side door and then the window for any signs of Dad. She went on "then there was another storm in March, about 1924, right after we were married. We got 8 to 10 inches of snow in one day. And now this storm, always in March. Where is your father? Maybe there are no buses running and he has to walk from the barber shop. Maybe something happened to him. What if he fell and is helpless in a snow bank.."

Finally, from a distance mother saw him, as did all of us who were watching for him as well. As he came closer, it was clear that he was carrying heavy bags of groceries in each arm. Finally he arrived at the side door - obviously worn out by the ordeal even for a man of forty-three years old. My mother looked into the bag and saw the chicken, produce, spaghetti, the Starwater, the Oxydol Detergent, the Octagon Soap with a free dish and dish towel included and said, "How much did these groceries cost?" My father said, "Seven dollars". "Seven dollars", my mother shouted, "I remember when we could get two bags for Five Dollars". With that my father turned his eyes toward heaven as he would often do and say something that sounded like "oof fah". "Oof fah" was the extent of my father's swearing and the expression would often follow when he would become exasperated with mother.

My mother's fears, as well as her old wives' tales, were immense. Most of these apprehensions were learned from her mother. One major fear was of lightning - not something to be taken lightly I understand. But when the lightning came to Mill Plain in the 1930's it was a moment for the gathering of all the children. We were ordered into the den which had no windows, lights were turned off, and there we were told to huddle together until it (the lightning) was over. My mother shook with each clap of thunder. I know that I for one would holler, "Mom, is it going to get us?"

There were other lessons learned from the 1930's. Some were strange lessons and were never cleared up. One day as we passed by a house where an old woman had died, my sister Lena said that the woman died and turned to stone or turned to stone and died -one or the other. Now since Lena more than likely heard that from someone older I would like to know what disease or illness did this poor old woman have that in 1930's gossip would so state that she turned to stone.

A lesson learned, however, before all others was that my father was to be listened to and by his authority, my mother as well. Over the years Junior and I would test my mother many times but never my father. My father used a distinct three notes whistle to summon us. When he whistled, we came. The whistle was only given once and we had to be within hearing distance or had to have received permission to be beyond the hearing of that call.

When we visited other homes which was a rarity, we all sat quietly in the corner and refused everything offered. When others spoke to us, we responded with manners or else. At school, the teacher was in charge and we obeyed.

In September, 1938, My sister Lena had a fourteenth birthday party. She invited a number of her first year high school friends. The next morning my father was angry. He called Lena to an apple tree and there he showed her the tree on which there were about twenty apples each with a bite taken out. "I'm going to talk with each of the parents and have them bring their son over (it had to be a boy) to check the size of the teeth marks" Lena was about to die of the potential embarrassment as was her close friend, Dorothy Cook. Boys would be asked to put their teeth into a partially bitten apple - a scene that would destroy Lena socially for the next four years of her high school careers. The threat never materialized. I never asked my father if he were serious. Even years later when we established a close relationship and I could talk with him openly, I never asked.

At times, reason went out the window as Junior and I tried to obey and respond. On one occasion, when I was about five and Junior about seven, I came up with a great idea to stop Mom from getting upset with us when we took our bath, always together. Mom left us in the tub with the usual admonition to wash behind our ears and between our legs. We in turn when taking our bath would invariably splash water onto the bathroom floor. This situation would bring out a major scolding and carrying on by my mother. On one of the bath nights, I said to Junior let's get all the towels out of the closet and put them on the floor so no water would be on the floor and Mom will not be mad at us. We undertook our great plan. Mom came in to check on us and she saw the sight of every clean towel laid neatly and slightly overlapping to be sure that no water was on the floor. "Oh no, Jesus, Mary, and Joseph help me. What am I going to do with these two. Angelo, Angelo come up here. I sweat bullets (a favorite expression) to keep this house immaculate and for what." Then she began to cry. Junior and I were in shock and terribly upset for causing our mother to be so angry . We tried to help and it turned out to be a disaster.

Mom had her hands full with the two of us - for sure. She was dramatic in terms of her reactions to the problems we would cause. Mom's usual reaction over the years was that she was going to put her head into the oven and then we'd see how it was like to be without a mother. Eventually, Junior and I knew that the threat was coming and we never interpreted her threat as too serious. But it had a reasonable effect for a short period of time and then we would forget the consequences prior to our next misbehavior.

I was invited for the first time to a birthday party when about five years old. The party was for a boy in my kindergarten class. My mother told me to be home at four o'clock. At five minutes to four, no presents were open and no cake was cut. But I dutifully went up to the boy's mother and told her that I had to leave in order to be home on time. It was a matter of discipline and how we were raised. It was not always logical but it was what we knew and understood.

It was also in Kindergarten that a game the teachers were teaching us to play made it apparent that I had an eye problem. When I arrived home, I asked my older brother and sister to teach me to eye up a target with each eye. First the right eye was tested with my finger extended and then the left eye. That is when I told them that my left eye was not working. Mom had Lena take me to the eye doctor just to the right of Apothecary Hall. The doctor had me read charts and found that the big E was not readable by me. As Lena and I walked home, she whistled using the card from the doctor with his diagnosis as her aide. If she was using the card as a whistle, then I must be okay. Unfortunately such was not the case. Thus began my seven year travail as a black-patched after school player. For two hours each day five days per week, I wore that black patch "so that my left eye will learn to follow my right" and for the record it worked. An eye that was beginning to weaken with lack of use began to follow with only an imperceptible trace of wandering. He was a smart doctor for what might be called early medicine. The doctor visit also meant eyeglasses. One eye lens was like the proverbial coke bottle and the other clear glass. So at times when playing I was called the "little professor", after Dom DiMaggio. I even began to turn my back slightly to home plate in the style of the Red Sox centerfielder. Eventually, doctors told me the eye had a congenital cause or possibly the result of a babyhood illness and was not repairable. In any case when confronted with the fact that I never became a great athlete, I usually blamed it on the "eye" and my ego was at rest.

My life long hero worship also began in the summer of 1939. In May of that year, I saw a Life magazine cover in Kresge's 5 and 10 cent store of Joe DiMaggio. My brother Lou was already a Yankee fan and I began to follow in his footsteps. It became a daily ritual to check the box score on the Yankees to see what Joe did the previous day and to cut out any pictures for my new scrapbook. I recall his injury in 1939 and his one month layoff returning in time to help the Yankees to their fourth straight American League title. He batted .381 that year with 30 home runs and had a slugging percent of .671. Typically, he rarely struck out.

Two things occurred on September 1, 1939. The first event did not yet have the sense of immediacy but the next day the morning headlines read that the German army had invaded Poland. A word that was new in the language and difficult to say and understand became part of the news. The Germans used a Blitzkrieg method of lightning warfare to invade Poland. Shortly after that invasion the newspaper reported, "Great Britain true to its pledge of aid to Poland, declared war on Germany". France followed with a declaration of war. Russia allied itself with the Germans and began to divide Poland into territorial control. To a six year old, the headlines were a mystery of sorts with the obvious questions as to why such events would occur and why would one country "invade" another. But from the limited point of view of a six year old, the invasion seemed to have little immediate effect upon my family or our neighbors.

The second event was of great importance to our family only. Aunt Anna, who was my father's sister, gave a birthday party for her daughter Beverly. Junior and I were invited. Aunt Anna lived on Orange Street in Waterbury. Her flat was on the third floor. During that night, from the outside porch of the flat, my brother and I began to exchange jeers and smart remarks with the locals who were playing below in the street. At the time we did not know it but in a few months, these boys would become our closest friends.

The world of 335 Atwood Avenue began to crumble in late 1939. At first, it was not perceptible. Occasionally, we would see my mother crying and when we would say, "Mom, why are you crying?" she would answer that it was okay and everything was all right. But the crying continued.

As a barbers' union organizer as well as an every day barber and Secretary-Treasurer of the Barbers' Union for over ten years, my father was a union man. It seemed somewhat in conflict that he was also an extremely active member of the Republican Party in and around Connecticut. He was not an FDR fan. As the events of the fall and winter of 1939 unfolded, it was clear that Dad had no love for the New Deal and the promises FDR made. My parents were about to lose their home. It was in his mind a direct relationship. We were losing our home because of lack of funds for mortgage payments and the FDR promises of help to offset mortgage foreclosure were not forthcoming. We were losing our home because the Democratic support of unionism and a living wage did not embrace the barbers.

Saturday, December 9, 1939 was a day typical for December in Connecticut. Icy sheets of snow lay upon the ground in patterns - snow, mud, and snow again. Connecticut winters, especially as the wind blew off the Sound, were typically cold but not necessarily snowy. The snow, when it came, piled high into drifts and then slowly melted forming seemingly never ending patterns of ice and mud and ice again. Today, the snow had hardened on the ground and the patches of ice and mud formed a criss-cross pattern across the vacant lot next to the house. Men in uniform came to the side door. They issued some papers and then two other men, movers, entered the house and began to take out the furniture. They placed the furniture on the snow and the mud in what appeared to be a strange pattern of statues on the barren ground. Placed at intervals were a mahogany table with matching chairs, a china closet, bed posts, and mattresses protected from the elements by blankets wrapped around them. This day was our day of eviction. Efforts to pay some of the back mortgage payments had not been successful. The dream was dying in front of my mother. Mrs. Sistilli came from across the street toward the house. She carried a pot of coffee the steam from which rose in the cold air. Tears rolled onto her cheeks. My mother was in the kitchen, trying to both supervise the movers and to find a way to make bread and butter sandwiches for her children. She wiped away tears from her own cheeks. My sisters, standing by, cried. Sam Sistilli who always wore his soldier pants from the War came to look and to offer sympathy by his presence. Mrs. Pennington, our neighbor from across the street, watched in disbelief. Neighbors stared dazed by things that were difficult to understand. How in this place with the love and belief in America that was so much a part of my mother's and father's life did this moment in time occur?

"Please Albina, sit down for just a moment and have a cup of hot coffee. It will do you good", Mrs. Sistilli said hoping for one more moment for the friends to be together. She had been a good friend and neighbor, loyal and trusted. "Will you be all right? Do you need anything?" Questions in rapid order to convey grief, concern, and love of neighbor.

Mom answered, "I'll, we'll be fine. I just don't understand why it is us. We've tried. We have never been dishonest or unfair or hurt anyone." Tears again began to emerge. The two women sat. Each with thoughts that provided some comfort. One with a quiet rage managed by years of self-control. The neighbor feeling a helplessness and a sense of inadequacy because the right words of comfort seemed beyond her.

Mom, with that show of inner strength that carried her through all misfortunes and disappointments, walked toward the movers. She gave directions to settle the affairs of transporting the last remnants of what was once her comfortable existence.

Within, there may have been a mournful wale, but it would not surface. She had to keep her children from the despair which she felt.

In actuality, the inevitable loss of home had become a reality long before the 9th of December. What we as children did not know is that six months of efforts to ward off the foreclosure were fruitless and a one story flat at 230 Orange Street awaited us.

The days of parades, company coming, and parties were over. What faced my mother and father was a struggle which led to a vow to leave Connecticut when the first opportunity arose. The dream of Mill Plain had disintegrated.

Chapter Four

A Time for Adjustment

On December 9, 1939, we moved into the first floor of a three story flat at 230 Orange Street. The flat consisted of five rooms - a kitchen, dining room, two bedrooms, a parlor and one bathroom. Tessie and Lena slept in one bed in one bedroom, Mom and Dad slept in the other bedroom. Lou, Junior and I slept in the parlor in two twin beds. Junior and I were in one bed and Lou slept in the other. The dining room was rarely used. A hallway was the entrance from the front porch into the dining room. In the hallway was the piano. We ate all of our meals at the kitchen table. The kitchen was large. a black iron oil stove for heating and cooking took up a large portion of one side of the room. Next to the stove was the gas water heater that had to be lighted in order to produce hot water. At one end of the kitchen was a walk-in pantry. The only bathroom was available through the kitchen or Mom and Dad's bedroom. Whenever, I had to go to the bathroom at night, I would head through Mom and Dad's bedroom and announce to my mother in her sleep that I was using the toilet.

The use of one bathroom was a major logistics problem. With five people trying to get ready for school and Dad trying to get ready for work, a schedule was necessary. Dad took the best way out. He left for work early in order to shave and take care of morning ablutions at his barber shop. For the rest of us, it was who had priority, and the two sisters had it. They would be up first to take care of all the needs that come with being female. Lou was next and then came Junior and me . The bath tub sat on legs and off the floor. The toilet had a water closet above the toilet which was activated by pulling the chain in a downward motion from the water closet. Mom would give a regular admonishment, "Don't forget to pull the chain!" Water for baths was heated by lighting the round cast iron boiler. When the match was struck, the burners would explode into flames that heated the water tank quickly. Any adjustment in the water temperature occurred by mixing the separate cold tap water and the extremely hot tap water to obtain a bearable temperature.

The house sat up from the street. At the first level was a wall about six feet high. Then a small patch of dirt which led to three or four steps onto a porch. On one side of the porch were two doors. The door on the right led into our flat and the door on the left led to the second and third levels. The second and third floor also had verandahs although the verandah on the third floor was smaller. The house was covered in an tarred type shingle that provided a sort of blanket during the winter and some protection from the heat in the summer. The back yard had no fence but after several feet from the back porch there was a slope that rose through an empty lot onto Dikeman Street. That flat became home for the next six years.

On the second floor was a young couple, Italian, with two babies. On the third floor were the "Russians" Jake and his wife. Jake owned the three story house and it was to him that I delivered on the first of each month, as was my job, an amount in cash of $28, the month's rent.

The Russians had a boarder. He was a Polish man who worked at the Chase Brass and Copper Company. Each Friday payday, he would begin drinking and come home each night of the weekend hardly able to stand. On a number of occasions, he would mistakenly choose the wrong entry door and come into our house. His door and our door were close together and doors in 1940's Waterbury were rarely locked. He would say something in Polish, we think an apology, and then stumble up two flights of stairs to his flat.

In the house next door to us were the Nishibecki's - also Polish. The father appeared to be a firm but kind man. The Nishibecki's had two sons, Walter and Eddie, who became part of the Hobo Jr.'s. of Orange Street.

On the other side were the Evans (pronounced Yvonnes). They had a son Alfred who was a member of our group. Alfred would see some one with food and would declare "halves" expecting that person automatically to give him half of whatever it was being eaten.

The Armstrong's lived on the corner. Their son, Richard, was a member of the group. He was the boy that could bring the bats and gloves.

The Williams, who lived across the street and down a block had several children. A son, Henry, had a glove and a bat. In addition, he was capable of playing well. There were an assortment of other boys who did not live on Orange Street but constituted a part of the Hobo Jr.'s. These boys included John Longo, who, like his name, was long in body. Danny Perragini, who lived on Wood Street, was also a member of the group.

Directly across the street lived Sonny Pestone, who was my age and was a good friend, although it was a chore to coax him to play sports or other street games. Sonny was the third child of a family of three children. He had an older brother and sister. Those three children were named for two older brothers and one sister who were hit and killed by lightning when standing near a tree on their way home from school. As the next three children were born, each was named for one of the dead children. Sonny told me that story once after I had known him a few years and the story made me feel uncomfortable.

The Pestone's were on the same party line as the Possemato's. At a precise moment, Sonny and I would pick up our phones and talk over the buzz that occurs with a phone off the hook. It was a simple attempt to beat the system.

The last two Hobo Jr.'s. were my brother Junior and I. Thus we had a baseball team plus one. When it was just street games, it was just the eight Orange Street group. The entire group was Irish, French, Polish, and Italian. There were no Jewish or Black kids in our group. The only Jewish family on Orange Street lived at the bottom of the hill. The family had one daughter who wore high top shoes. She had hair combed straight down and cut just below the ears. Her hair was parted on the side. She wore a bow just below the part. My mother said that they were poor. From then on, until I learned otherwise upon moving to California, I though all Jewish people were poor. At least I thought, they were poorer than Italians.

Blacks lived one street down and remained separate from us during the after school hours and on weekends.

My sister, Tessie, Junior, and I attended Walsh Grammar School. Lou was permitted to continue the 1939-40 year (his 8th and final year) at Chase Grammar School before going to Crosby High School to join his sister Lena who was a sophomore in school year 1939-40.

Walsh Grammar School was becoming a mix of European ethnic groups and Blacks during the early 1940's. Blacks were being recruited out of the south to work in the factories as government sponsored manufacturing programs began to stimulate the economy. The government programs were initiated to build parts and to make critical materials for England and later Russia in their struggles with Germany.

My recollections of Blacks are many and varied. Lois Carnes was a pretty light skinned Black girl who, in the cloak room at recess, liked to raise her dress and show her panties. On Valentine's Day, it was traditional for each member of the class to put a valentine in the box for each member of the class. I bought a packet which contained 28 friendship valentines. There were 29 students in my class. I made out 28 cards the night before and told my brother Junior that I did not have a card for Lois. He told me that I was going to the store now and buy one more card and make sure that Lois got her card. I did and she did. To this day, I believe that Lois was not going to receive a card because she was always raising her dress. It could not have been because she was Black because other Black kids in my class received a card from me. But I often wondered.

Charley was a janitor at one of the factories. Charley always had on his janitor's uniform when he helped us with some of the fundamentals of baseball. He was knowledgeable and talented and he liked us. Charley was a medium dark Black. He laughed a lot and talked to us as if we were smart too. We had an ongoing complaint to Charlie that the baseball hurt when it hit the bone just below the index finger. One day, Charley told us that if we wanted to catch a baseball and not have it hurt we had to take a certain measure. Charley said, "Boys you have got to pee on your hand that catches the ball and if you do this often enough your hand will toughen up". To this day, I don't know whether Charley was kidding or was serious. I tried to pee on my hand once but didn't like the idea and so I stopped. My hand continued to hurt when I caught the ball.

Joe Louis was the hero to many people but especially to Blacks of the 1940's. As Louis won another fight, Black boys at school would bob and weave in front of us in a fighting pose as they threw left and a right jabs and would say, "You better not mess with me because my uncle is Joe Louis".

During one spring day in about 1943, I was walking home across the playground and saw a group of Blacks circled around what appeared to be a fight. When I got through the crowd, I saw my sister, Tessie, getting up from the ground. She was next to a Black girl who looked as if her blouse was torn. Tessie was bloodied but unbowed although she looked a bit like she may have gotten the worst of it. I walked home behind her never speaking of the fight to her, or asking whether she won, lost, got beat up, or punched. I never told my parents about the fight. If she wanted to tell them that was up to her.

During the summers, Junior and I would always wear shorts, socks, and sneakers - no tops. My father always cut our hair very short in the summer. The consequences of which were that the two of us roamed Orange Street and our coloring grew darker than tan. In fact, with the sun adding to our olive skin, we were definitely on the dark side. One day, we went to the corner store for some groceries for my mother. A Black woman was in the store and she began to look at us - up and down and then up and down again. Finally, she turned to Junior and in a serious manner said, "Boy, tell me something. Are you two white boys or are you two Black boys?" "We're white! We're white", said my brother as quickly as he could get it out. And then she laughed - a big laugh - so we weren't sure whether she was serious or kidding with us.

As a way of summing up about the relationships regarding Blacks in the 1940's in Waterbury, my recollections are that Blacks and whites did not have major problems in their relationships. I can not recall one incident of a clash between Blacks and whites as occurred in other cities. My memories are positive especially when I think of the older Black women that I encountered over those early years. This memory is quite simplistic but it is how I remember it. Black women seemed to love children no matter what color, were very friendly, and, as best I can put it, joyful in spirit.

In 1937, my father expanded his barber shop at 50 Bank Street in downtown Waterbury by adding a beauty shop. The business became Jo-An's Beauty and Barber Shoppe.

A flier that advertised the services at Jo-An's Beauty Shoppe began with message:

Jo-An's Beauty Shoppe

50 Bank Street Waterbury, Conn. Tele: 5-1171

Dear Miss or Madam:

Does you hair need our attention.

Then Dial 5-1171.

The message went on to ensure that a Jo-An's permanent was guaranteed. Prices for machine type permanents went from $3.00 to $8.50 or for non-machine type from $4.00 to $10.00. In the bottom half of the flyer, the same message was repeated in Italian.

The beauticians employed at Jo-An's were Lucille Mackowitz (referred to in the flyer as Lucille Mack); Mafalda Colangelo; and

Sylvia Juliano. These three beauticians were the original work force for Jo-An's. Eventually the shop expanded in size by doubling its floor space and including two floors. The shop was remodeled with modern equipment installed. A newspaper article on places of business in and around Waterbury described Jo-An's as "the center of individualistic hair creations".

In its first operating year, Dad reported on the tax form that the shop had a gross of $5,204 and a cost of operations of $3,802. Thus it showed a gross profit of $1,402. After expenses were deducted from the gross profit, the shop lost $1,043. During the second year, the business grew to $8,000 gross income and began to meet its expenses.

Each Friday, all beauticians, eventually the number reached eight, received their paycheck first, as did my father's partner, Joseph Capella. The remainder, after rents and utilities were paid, was my father's salary. The beauticians received between $45 and $75 per month depending on the business, not counting tips. In the best months, Joseph Cappella took home about $70 and Dad about $80 to $100 per month.

Joseph Capella was the husband of my mother's sister, Mary. He, like many other of my father's personal and barber friends, was born in Benevento, Italy. Family history has it that he had a continuing fondness for women. His customers were taken by his unusual good looks. He had the appearance of what may be called a swarthy Italian. He had dark hair parted just off center and slicked back. His complexion was olive. He was in good shape and enjoyed the attention that women gave him. In turn, he responded to that attention. It is also important to mention that he had a flair when working with women's hair and was the reason for the general soundness of the woman's side of the business during years when women spending money on hairdo's was a luxury.

My father would also give permanents but mainly took care of the men's side of the shop-supervising other barbers and providing haircuts and shaves to his male customers.

During the late 1930's and into 1940 my father continued to be active in Republican political affairs, the barbers' union, and veteran's affairs. In 1940, he accepted the bid to run for the State Assembly as a Republican. My own diligence in the 1940 election is remembered with fondness. First, because it was the beginning of a life-long love of politics and, as well, the reading of the newspaper - especially the letters to the editors and the editorial page. My interest in the politics of the City of Waterbury, the State of Connecticut, the nation, and ultimately the world, took shape by my reading the newspaper on the kitchen floor which became my desk throughout grammar school.

There was a ramp from Dikeman Street to the basement of Walsh Grammar School, and it was that route which voters took to the polling place on the school grounds. I brought a number of buttons to school with "Out! Stealing Third". The button was in green print on a white background. On another button was a picture of Wendell Wilkie and the words "One World". On a third buttons which I distributed were the words "Baldwin for Governor" with a picture of an apple. I also recall reading an article by Thomas E. Dewey about the time of the election. Dewey charged that the Roosevelt attempt to gain a third term was a dangerous threat against liberty. I'm not sure how I got away with politicking near a polling booth without anyone stopping me. Maybe I was viewed as a bit of a nuisance and little else.

My father's campaign was a straight Republican ticket approach. The Waterbury American newspaper ran a political advertisement with the heading "Be Sure to Pull the Second Lever and Vote the Straight Republican Ticket". A slate was running - Maurice P. Wrenn for Judge Probate, Franklyn Barringer for State Senator, Edward Mraz for State Representative, Harold Post for State Senator, and Angelo Possemato for State Representative. In that same paper was an announcement for "Political Broadcasts" which said that Angelo Possemato would speak at 8:00 p.m. on WBRY radio. I listened to my father's talk. As reported in the October 24, 1940 issue of the Waterbury paper, candidate Possemato said in part, "Labor will find in me a friend who understands labor problems and a man willing to support just legislation in their behalf. As a veteran, I promise to place my country and state above...political affiliation. Dad also assailed the New Deals attempt to break tradition in seeking a third term and its attempt to take credit for jobs created pointing out that there are still nine million people looking for work, the same number as when FDR took office. In any case, my father lost the election. Republicans did not do well in the FDR/Wallace and Democratic landslide that buried the Wilkie/McNary ticket and many Republicans along the way. The election results in Waterbury were similar to 1932 and 1936 with about 60% of the voters choosing a Democrat over a Republican. But I had a wonderful first taste of politics. In retrospect, it could be concluded that Dad had his greatest opportunity to win statewide office in the late 1920's and early 1930's when his name was closely associated with the union and veteran movements in Waterbury. By the 1940 election, he was forty five years old and much of his battles for unionizing the barbers and making the veterans a strong voice in politics was lost due in large part the growing trauma of a world war.

At least, 1940 was a good year for DiMaggio even if it was Detroit's year to win the American League pennant. Joe led the league in hitting with a .352 batting average and had 133 runs batted in. Again typically, he rarely struck out.

An important event in my life in 1941 was my Catechism instructions. My need to never be embarrassed when required to perform in any matter was both a blessing and a curse to me. The catechism class was being instructed by an older priest, probably well into his sixties at the time, who was also the pastor of St. Mary's which we now attended. He would drill the class unceasingly for about 90 minutes once a week. My need was to memorize all prayers perfectly and the catechism as well. Each time he called on me, which I felt was too often, I would answer word for word right out of the book. When a student did not answer correctly, he would open his book and say "that is a zero entered by your name". I had no zeros for the twenty weeks of the instruction. On the day which was the last of our instructional meetings, he said, "Paul, stand up." He then proceeded to ask me a question from the first lesson. With perfect response, I answered him. It was a triumph of sorts for what was and still is an ego and a pride which over the years has been both a strength and a major flaw in my character. It was a game and I knew what rules were being played by the priest and because I wanted to play I was determined to win.

As it occurred for each of my two brothers and me, communion meant buying a black suit from the wholesaler on East Main Street.. On rack after rack, the tailor had suits - all black - and in all sizes. Do you want black or black? The suits were all made from a heavy wool material that sagged and smelled in the rain. The cost for the suit was $5 for my size. The tailor also carried racks of camel hair coats. They cost $10 and were beautiful, sporty, and well beyond our means.

A positive event occurred from those communion lessons however was that the pastor permitted me to make my Confirmation with the twelve year olds during the spring of 1942. So as an eight year old, I was confirmed. Well, I have records to prove I was confirmed. But going through the ceremony was a different matter. On the Sunday morning of the Confirmation ceremony with the Bishop coming to preside, Junior and I went to the 10:00 a.m. mass. At the end of mass, during the announcements, the priest said now please no one leave because we will have the Confirmation ceremony immediately following the mass. I got up to leave to join the others being confirmed, but Junior held me and would not let me get up. Junior said, "Didn't you hear the priest no one leaves?" I say, "But I have to get in line". Junior said, "You are not going". So, I watched the class file down receive the blessing from the bishop while I looked on. Did I lose my Confirmation on a technicality?

The indifference toward the war in Europe began to end in the Spring of 1940. It is my estimate that schoolchildren of the early 1940's became excellent geography students because of the war in Europe and Asia and the resulting approach by teachers to trace the major occurrences with a map and with a geography lesson.

In April, 1940, Hitler invaded Norway and Denmark. Denmark capitulated and Norway declared war on Germany. Thus began the rolling down of the map and the questions as to where is Norway? Denmark? Where were the British pushed back into the sea in Norway? John (or Mary or Jane or) come show us on the map. Here use my pointer. "Very good!" or "No, a little to your left. That's it, good". Thus began one of the longest lessons in geography lasting over six years until the war had ended.

In May, 1940, Hitler sent troops into Belgium, the Netherlands, and Luxembourg. The Dutch were overwhelmed and surrendered in less than a week. The Wehrmacht drove through Belgium to the English Channel. King Leopold surrendered the entire Belgium army. But 400,000 British troops were evacuated from Dunkerque. Teachers told us of the bravery of every day citizens who risked their lives to evacuate the British by small boats, trawlers, and whatever means that they could muster to save the British force from annihilation.

In June, 1940, Germans marched into Paris. Paris!! Teachers who told us of their visits to Paris during previous summers cried as they talked about the breaking of the Magino Line and the surrender of Paris. There was no sympathy for Marshall Petain whom they called a traitor for signing an armistice giving Germany about one-half of France including Paris. Petain called for the need to" recreate lost confidence".

As they explained, we watched the blitzkrieg through the eyes of the teachers and by way of our wall maps.

In July 1940, three countries became part of the news that we had only heard about because some friend or relative was born there and had came to the United States. We learned that Estonia, Latvia, and Lithuania were annexed by the Russians. The names Estonia, Latvia, and Lithuania for the rest of the war years were always linked in one breath as if they were one place.

In that same month, the British attacked French warships and Petain severed relations with the British. The class went to sea and began following the war on the ocean front as well.

One of the most memorable events occurred in August, 1940 when Nazi Luftwaffe (a new term for students) began the bombing of Britain. These events became especially poignant when the newsreels at the Saturday matinee showed the destruction that an aerial attack can generate on a city and its people. I remember the future Queen Elizabeth as a young girl in some type of uniform standing by an army truck. I can not remember exactly what she was doing but she was a part of the war effort. Another scene of great impact showed British children being sent to the country so as to avoid the bombings.

The Italians entered the war on the side of the Axis by invading British Somaliland in August 1940. The British repelled the attack and took significant number of Italian prisoners. A whole new area of the world - Africa - became part of our classroom lessons.

In October, 1940, Italy invaded Greece assisted by the Germans.

In November, 1940, Slovokia, Hungary, and Romania joined the Axis powers.

In January, 1941, Germany and Russia signed a new friendship pact.

In March, 1941, Yugoslavia joined the axis; however, three weeks after the pact was signed, Hitler ordered the invasion of Yugoslavia and the country surrendered.

One of the strangest events of the war occurred in May, 1941 when Rudolph Hess, Hitler's aide, parachuted into Scotland to offer an alleged peace agreement to the British. Rudolph Hess had a powerful looking face with a wide jaw and bushy eyebrows that seemed to present a permanent scowl. He was as threatening as any image of the Nazi.

In May, 1941, I became a newspaper boy with my own paper route. The distributor would pick up about eight paper carriers at the bottom of Wood Street. We would ride to our beginning spot to start our route by sitting on his fenders and holding on to the front headlights or we would ride by standing on the running board and holding on to the window column. My route started in the middle of Walnut Street and continued along Rose, Woods, Ives, Irion, Oak, and Beach Streets. Each paper boys carried a canvas paper sack. As I walked, I would fold the papers several times and tuck the folded end in so as to make a package of about three inches wide. Then the task was to deliver the paper by throwing it to a front porch or up two or three stories to a verandah. We had about 60 customers and the job took about an hour and a half each day - Monday through Saturday. Once each month we would knock on doors to be paid. About 90% went to the distributor and 10% was kept by the paper boys. I kept this job for the four years of the war. I believe my take for each month was a little over $4.00.

On June 2, 1941, the paper boys were waiting on the corner for our pickup when a man came by and told us that Lou Gehrig had died. Lou Gehrig! Impossible! He was the Iron Man - a hero to us. The Yankees were our team and Lou Gehrig had been an important player through pennant and World Series wins. He was the unassuming and quiet hero. He played in the shadow of Babe Ruth and was still a superstar. He could not have died, but he did. We talked about it. It was a difficult moment. Later one of the paper boys said that he read that he died of a disease that cripples. Another said that it paralyzed him so that he could not walk, speak, or move his arms. How could anyone so talented as an athlete become so crippled. His death and the disease that killed him had a profound effect upon us.

In June 1941 another event that was difficult to understand from the perspective of a seven year old occurred. It was the declaration of war on Russia by Germany, Italy, and Romania. I thought that they were friends. Not likely, as German troops invaded Russian borders. Finland still upset at the Russian takeover earlier joined the Axis against Russia.

With the invasion of Russia by the Germans, the Russians and British, in July, 1941, signed a joint action against Germany . On July 3, 1941, Stalin called for the citizens of Russia to defend their land and their soil.

President Roosevelt met with Winston Churchill in the Mid-Atlantic on board a battleship and signed the Atlantic Charter guaranteeing the four freedoms.

In that same month, Britain invaded Iran.

The 1941 baseball year was a great one for the Yankees and DiMaggio. The Yankees won the American League pennant again. DiMaggio led the league in runs batted in at 125 but most importantly he batted .357 and hit safely in 56 straight games. The streak began May 15, 1941 and continued for 3 months and 2 days. He broke George Sisler's mark on June 29th with his 42nd hit. Next came Wee Willie Keeler's mark of 44 consecutive game hits. His streak ended at 56 games on July 17, 1941 against the Cleveland Indians. He batted .408 during the stretch. In 1941, Ted Williams won the batting title with a .406 mark. Joe finished third in the batting race - two points behind Cecil Travis of the Senators. Joe DiMaggio was more than just a ballplayer and a Yankee. He was an Italian-American and a source of tremendous pride not only for his ability but also for the manner by which he presented himself both on and off the field.

In October, 1941 Joe DiMaggio became a father with the birth of Joe Jr. to him and his wife Dorothy Arnold DiMaggio. For some reason, we felt good and celebrated that maybe a future Yankee Clipper was born.

In October, 1941, the Germans advanced through Russia quickly and soon held Moscow in a state of siege.

It was about that time that we began to learn the term "Mother Russia" from the teachers. They showed us charts of temperature drops and of the cold Russian winters. The Germans were unable to sustain their supply lines into Russia. We charted the distances from the German border to the German front in Russia. We combined that information with the temperature charts and concluded, with teacher help, the difficulty of such a supply route. Teacher told us of another attempt to conquer Russia by Napoleon and the lack of success which he had due to the same circumstances. In November, 1941 the Russians began a counter-offensive at Rostov which in effect began the demise of the Germans on their eastern front.

There were other remembrances during the months and years before the United States entry into the war. These events had an impact in later years. One such discussion from a science fiction magazine was the possibility of a machine that could do complex and multiple mathematics problems in record time. Such a machine, it was predicted, would eventually eliminate the need for such things as pencil and paper census taking and mathematical equations by hand. Another was a machine that would eventually be able to transmit pictures from one place to another by air waves. A third was the development of nylon. Nylon first appeared at the 1939 World's Fair in New York. The Fair was memorable for its symbol which consisted of a golden structure that had two parts - a tall and tapered sharply edged obelisk with a large round ball placed next to it. My mother talked about nylon with her sisters, with Tessie and Lena, and with neighbors. Nylon was stronger than silk and could be made into stockings for women. We didn't even imagine that in a few short months it would be the fabric of parachutes for the airborne troops.

Another remembrance was that of a squadron of gray cars with an circle emblem of red and white on the side of the car. Part of the red in the symbol was above the 1/2 way point of the circle and part of the red was below the 1/2 way point. On the side of the car were the words "Join Technocracy Now". What was Technocracy? One day I had the courage to ask a driver of one of the cars about the name and the symbol. He said that technocracy people were devoted to the belief that technical experts are more capable of running government than the average person. At the dawn of an age of what is now called the Technology Age, the Join Technocracy Now forces wanted a society ran by experts who were technical in nature and capable. As the war came, Technocracy as an organization and a philosophy faded.

For my part, I dreamed of being able to go to the movies on Sunday and come home to listen to my radio which somehow captured within it the radio shows that I missed while at the movies. I wanted to hear on my time "The Shadow" to name one such favorite.

For most Americans the bottom of the depression may have been the year 1933, but for many Americans, little evidence was present in the late 1930's to show that gains were occurring in their level of living. Our family reflected that lack of success in any slow climb out of poverty. The flat on Orange Street was too small for a family of seven, but it was home and we were a close family.

The years between 1939 and the entry of the United States into World War II were a mix of both hope and despair for Americans. Businesses slowly began to emerge from the depression's devastating hole of bankruptcy, unemployment, and low productivity. With the beginnings of the United States involvement as an arsenal and a manufacturer for the nations of Europe, Americans began to feel that the burdens of poverty and unemployment may be coming to an end. Money was limited but there arose a feeling that the next few years were only an interim step for better things that were ahead. At least we hoped so. Most Americans did not sense the imminent threat of involvement and did not anticipate that the United States would soon not only be a manufacturer of war goods but an actual participant in a devastating four years of warfare.

Chapter Five

The War Comes

As was a routine on Sunday afternoons, Junior and I were on our way to either the Loew's Poli or the State movie house with our friends. As usual we walked down Maple Avenue and past 108 Maple where my Grandmother and Grandfather Mocciola lived. Each Sunday, they would be sitting by the upstairs window talking with neighbors who passed by.

As we passed, Grandma would say, "Junior, Paulie come up and have some tea." The words were always pronounced with a definite Italian accent so "some" as an example was "soma" and up was pronounced "upa". "No, Grandma we have to get to the show". "You come up and have some tea". "Yes Grandma". We did unfailingly.

We had tea with sugar and milk and Grandma would ask how Mama and Daddy were and brother and sisters. We would say fine. Grandma would say now "you do niceta niceta". "Niceta" was pronounced as three syllables. That meant that Junior and I should behave at all times - that is we should be nice, nice. When Grandma had finished admonishing us to be nice, we could go. Once in a great while, Grandma would say it's too hot for tea so she would give us something to make us cool and with that she would give us Pepsi-Cola and milk mixed together.

My Grandmother Mocciola had a difficult existence with Grandpa Mocciola. Sometime during the marriage, he decided that Grandma could not go to mass or to visit church. So in her backyard, she set up a shrine and each day in Latin she would say the mass and the rosary. I suppose that a part of her daily prayer ritual included passages for her husband so that he would see the light, but he never did. Grandma eventually was diagnosed with diabetes and her leg was amputated because of a gangrene infection. Four months after we moved to California, she died from the diabetes.

There was a picture painted of Grandma that I saw later that overwhelmed me. When we knew her, she had few teeth and was probably in her sixties. Not old by today's standards but quite old to us. But there in a bedroom in subsequent years, I saw this magnificent portrait of a young beautiful woman with a creamy white complexion, shiny black hair and green eyes. She was a woman a bit over 5 foot 7 inches tall. I recall her calling us for tea and I remember that picture and this beautiful woman and I am teary eyed.

Grandpa Mocciola was probably too mean to die young. He lived to be eighty-seven old, never changing his views that priests, the church, and religion were burdens to be shunned.

He also carried life burdens however. He needed an operation to remove a double hernia. But without funds, he suffered without an operation throughout his adult life. Grandpa took to wearing long dresses in public so as to ease the pain that the pants caused against his groin. He would walk around Waterbury with two shopping bags to and from the market. On several occasions, walking around the downtown area, my friends would point out, "There's your Grandpa in his woman's dress". We would acknowledge that it was he, made sure that we said hello to him, but left all other comments unsaid. A grandfather who treated Grandma so cruelly and walked around in such attire was a burden for the young.

On this particular Sunday, December 7, 1941, when we arrived home that afternoon after the movies, Mom and Dad were listening to the radio. Mother was crying. The Japanese had bombed Pearl Harbor. Word of our losses from the bombing was not precise. Many American service personnel had been killed. Ships were sinking. Smoke was overwhelming the workers trying to save lives. The reports stated that the United States Pacific fleet may have been lost due to the attack.

As the hours and days went by, the reports became clearer. The Japanese had destroyed over 300 planes and killed over 2,400 Americans. If there are monumental points of unification in American history, then Pearl Harbor must have been the most unifying of all. Very shortly, it was a revelation to watch the reconciling of the somewhat indifferent and scholarly approach to the European's war prior to December 7th with the fervor of patriotism that emerged as a result of the events of that December day. A stunned America came to realize that the deteriorating conditions between the United States and Japan for the last four or more years resulted in a sneak attack. Those were the words that were repeated often after that date, "Sneak Attack". These words represented the enemy who killed thousands of young Americans with a raid without warning.

On Monday, December 8th, I ran home from school at lunch time to hear the President speak before the Congress. I recall vividly his opening statement:

Yesterday, Dec. 7, 1941-a date which will live in infamy—the United States of America was suddenly and deliberately attacked by naval and air forces of the empire of Japan.

The United States was at peace with that nation, and...

The results of the Pearl Harbor attack were more devastating as information through the newspaper and radio became available. The US Nevada and the US Arizona were hit. The Arizona sank quickly and the US Nevada beached itself and as a result underwent a brutal bombardment. The US Raleigh, the US Utah, and the US Curtsies were damaged markedly. Hickam Field was badly damaged. Over 350 Japanese planes took part in the bombings.

The United States in December 1941 also declared war on Germany and Italy. There was some good news from the Russian front that winter month for the Russians announced that the Germans were in retreat on the entire eastern front.

Life changed for everyone. In many ways America history can be divided into major events - pre Revolution and post Revolution, pre Civil War and post Civil War, pre frontier movement and post frontier movement, pre immigration and post immigration, pre World War I and post World War I, pre depression and post depression, and pre World War II and post World War II. It may not have been evident at first but gradually the realization set in. Within months, words and ways of doing business entered the American psyche that were never there before and changed forever America and Americans.

On a more personal note, luck and good fortune did not yet arrive for the family. Because business was just sufficient to pay the payroll, supplies, and the utilities, Dad decided that he did not have enough money to pay for fire insurance. He held off on paying the premium. That decision cost him dearly. When luck is going poorly, it sometime takes a real nose dive, and it did. On January 8, 1942 just a few weeks after Pearl Harbor, Jo-An's Beauty and Barber Shop was lost in a fire that destroyed the building and the business.

The Waterbury American newspaper of January 9, 1942 ran the story with a picture of the shop's interior. The title above the picture was "Nature's Fingerwave Created in Bank Street Fire". The cold January weather turned the shop into a strange looking wonderland. Water from fire hoses froze to form icicles on permanent wave equipment, electrical lines, and furniture.

The fire removed the last possibility that good fortune would just bend a bit toward us. If there was any small inkling of changing one's mind about staying in Connecticut, it really was burned up in the embers at 50 Bank Street.

The newspaper that reported the fire also introduced a note of realism into the total scene. In the same newspaper was one the first stories regarding the impact that food shortages would have on shoppers during the war. The title of the story was "Hoarding, Not Scarcity, Blamed for Sugar Rationing".

A small remembrance came out of the fire's aftermath. Dad had to continue barbering to make a living so he opened a barber shop above the A&P Market about two blocks down from where fire occurred. On a Sunday soon after the opening, he had to clean the shop and took me along. I swept and cleaned and felt such a sense of pride for an eight year old.

The classroom geography instruction intensified as the war became America's priority. In January, 1942, American troops arrived in Ireland. Field Marshall Rommel stopped the British drive into Libya. Soon after, Singapore surrendered to Japanese forces after a 40 day battle.

On April 18, 1942, Lt. Col. James Doolittle flying low under cover, and with an air armada of 16 B-25 medium bombers took off from the aircraft carrier Hornet and headed for Japan. The raid was a tremendous lift for Americans. In the classroom, we celebrated an American victory. In the early days of the war, such a victory was rare.

In May 1942, the air raid battles intensified when the Royal Air Force (RAF) dropped 6,000,000 pounds of bombs on Cologne in the biggest air raid of the war to date. The British, recovering from earlier setbacks, pushed toward Tobruk in Libya.

In May, 1942, the government established the Women's Auxiliary Army Corps (WAAC's). Within one weekend after its establishment, the newsreel showed several women saluting and dressed in their newly designed WAAC uniforms. We had read that some women were flying planes in the Russian Army and so we asked our teacher whether American women would carry guns and fight.

The battle of the Coral Sea was another boost for Americans. In the classroom, we identified the area, the aircraft carriers that were involved, and celebrated the first defeat of the Japanese in the South Pacific. Then came Midway where Americans turned back the Japanese fleet with the sinking of four Japanese carriers.

One of the names to capture the imagination of grade school students was Vinegar Joseph Stilwell and his fighters who protected the building of new supply lines across Burma and thwarted Japanese efforts to reach India.

In August, 1942, US Marines invaded Guadacanal in the southern Solomons in order to stop Japanese efforts to reach Australia. The fighting went on for six months. The reports on the number of Marines killed were staggering but still we were proud of the type of courage that they showed and the hardships that they endured through the jungles of the Solomons.

Joe DiMaggio's last year playing for the Yankees before he entered the service was 1942. It was not one of his best years. He batted .305 with one of his lower slugging percentages of .498. The Yankees suffered a humiliating defeat in the World Series losing to the St. Louis Cardinals in four straight games. Yankee fans suffered. No fan believed that they were mortal.

Dad took the opportunity to serve again during the War. But this time in a different capacity than active duty. He became a night guard at a defense plant- wearing a uniform, carrying a badge, and a flashlight that looked like a two foot long blackjack, He attended defense training school in case any "saboteurs", as he said, tried to do harm to the factory. He brought home a jujitsu book and playfully, thankfully, practiced on Junior and me. He was very proud of a certificate he received from the United States of America, Army of the United States, *Certificate of Meritorious Conduct* as a member of the Auxiliary to the Military Police of the Army serving at The American Brass Company.

Even with Dad working two jobs and mother also working, there continued to be little money for any "luxury" expenditures - just bare necessities. One day my mother was saying again to me that the important thing was family not money and she added, "Money can't buy happiness". I said in all seriousness, "Well, can it at least buy us (and I began to spell out) the "h-a-p-p-i-" part of happiness". She looked at me and began to laugh - a long and full laugh. I realized that unknowingly I had made a joke and a rather good one so I laughed as well.

Despite the lack of money and the generally dire conditions, we were still a close knit family. It was not a democratic family. Dad was the boss, but on too many occasions, Junior and I challenged that authority. We found time to fight about something on a regular basis. My favorite way of antagonizing him was to say as nicely as I could, "Would you get——for me?" The——could be a book, or a glass of water, or a piece of paper whatever. When he brought it to me, I would say, "I made you do it". And that did it. I would start running and he would start chasing. Mom would say, "Stop fighting" or, "Wait until your father comes home". When my father came home, we would get a whack on the behind. In retrospect, I have great regret that we placed such a burden on my father. There were few men who were more gentle except when it came to the two of us. Our behavior was the last straw for the day. He would come home from working two shifts and Mom would give her report. Exasperation must have set in on many occasions. He used his hand against Mickie only once and never laid a hand on sister Tessie or older brother Lou, but Junior and I were another story.

Junior and I respected and feared our Dad but the fear was the anticipation of punishment which would occur after one more bad report from my mother. Relationships between Junior and me would be calm for a couple of weeks then something would trigger a fight all over. I contend that until my brother grew to be 6 foot and one inches tall and weighted 220 pounds, I could lick him. My sisters say that he would just laugh at me and not use full force.

There was one occasion for which, to this day, I am markedly ashamed of my actions. A few friends and I were walking down Orange Street on a Saturday in the early afternoon. Surprisingly, my father was walking up the hill. He apparently was coming home unexpectantly for lunch. I froze. My state of mind was the result of the previous day's behavior when I had angered him through one of my several misdeeds. As I walked by him, I said nothing. Later that afternoon, as I was playing on the street with a number of the neighborhood friends, he whistled that distinct whistle which means come here. I did. In front of my friends, he slapped me once on the face with one of his gloves. He said nothing and went up the stairs to the house. It was clear what I had done. I insulted him, and he let me know how an insult feels in front of my friends.

On another occasion, I pulled a blunder which was an insult to guests in our house, but I was innocent just stupid. My Mom and Dad were having a late dessert snack with my Uncle Dominic and Aunt Julia and some other of their friends whose names I have long since forgotten. We were all sitting at the kitchen table along with my sister, Tess, and my brother, Junior. Someone mentioned the cost of the cookies and how many one received in the package for the price paid. I, in all innocence, said, "Well, let's count how many were in the package." In order to accomplish the task, I counted how many were left in the package and then asked each person how many they had eaten. I then added the total and said that there were forty cookies for the price paid. My father said nothing. When all the guests left. He looked at me with the look that I knew. I was in trouble. "Don't you ever show such bad manners again by insulting our guests. Asking them how many cookies they had is bad manners and you were taught better." With that the back of his left hand came across my left cheek.

On the streets Junior and I were always together during those War years. Every night both before and after supper, we would be outside with the others on Orange Street. The games varied from "Johnny Jump the White Horse", "Drop the Handkerchief", "Kick the Can", "Red Rover". For the girls, playing at some distance, it was "double dutch", "Jacks", or "Hop Scotch". On Saturdays, it was baseball at the coal yards. On Sunday morning after church it was stick ball. Stick ball was a type of cricket and baseball rolled into one. One had to hit the tennis ball with a broom stick type bat and run to second base (the only base in the game) before it was fielded and you were thrown out. You were also out if the ball was caught in the air. Scoring consisted of your partner hitting you home.

The Hobo Jr.'s. modeled themselves after their older brothers, the Hobo's. The Hobo Jr.'s. played basketball in the YMCA League. We were terrible but game. On one Saturday, we were scheduled to play the first place team, but a scheduling problem meant that the YMCA floor was not available and the game had to be canceled. However, instead of rescheduling it, the leaders determined to give us a loss and the other team a win "because the Hobo Jr.'s wouldn't have won anyway". I suppose that is when my sense of justice and fair play emerged deeper than ever before. I was angry and went to the adults and argued that they couldn't just give us a loss without a game. They clearly thought that I was a nuisance and let the "loss" stand. Many experiences shape our sense of right and wrong and that experience was one of my most important ones.

In July, 1942, Uncle Dominic Possemato bought a new 1942 Oldsmobile two-door sedan. It was yellow and black with plastic instead of chrome bumpers. it was the last model year car to be built until the war was over. It cost $1,200.

In July, 1942, Nazi forces rolled into Egypt. In August, 1942, American rangers suffer heavy losses in a commando raid at Dieppe.

In September, 1942, Nazis moved in on Stalingrad but a Russian counter-offensive began.

In October, 1942, Mom went to work at the Clock Shop where once Waterbury watches were made, Now, the Shop was making precision instruments for the war effort, Mom did piece work making bomb sights. Her station was at the window that looked toward Camp Street.

One of the first major offensives of the war occurred in November, 1942. It was a day that lifted the spirits on Americans and the students in the classroom. British and American forces landed in Northwest Africa and captured Casablanca and Oran.

As the year lengthened, more and more banners appeared in windows. The banners were about 12 inches long and 8 inches wide. Each banner had a white field with a gold fringe as a border. On the banner were blue stars - one blue star for each son or daughter or husband in the service. Banners began to appear in windows with frequency. My Aunt Mary eventually had three stars in her banner representing her three sons serving in various armed services.

If a banner had a gold star, it meant that a son or daughter or husband had died in the War. Gold Star mothers organizations were formed - unfortunately with greater regularity. When the gold star went up, other mothers gathered at the home to offer what ever condolences one could give in such a time to the bereaving.

To address the growing need to deliver mail, the US Post office began delivery twice a day and on Saturdays. V-Mail also began. V-Mail was a means of writing on very thin like blue tinted tissue paper that folded. The outside of the paper was used as an envelope. Thus one piece of paper of very little weight produced a letter and an envelope.

The office of Price Administration was formed to maintain prices so that inflation would not eat up income. Chester Bowles became a household name. The message was that rationing could ease shortages but not prevent them entirely. Consumers had to be protected from retailers who would want to capitalize on the needs of the public by unfairly raising prices.

In October, 1942, students in the classroom became aware of British General Bernard L. Montgomery whose forces struck Axis lines at El Alamein. That drive began the push of the Germans out of North Africa. We traced his advances on our wall maps.

In December, 1942, gasoline rationing began.

Jobs were readily available for young men and women as the adult male labor force went off to war. Brother Lou got a job delivering milk in the mornings before school. Milk was delivered on doorsteps with a pre-arranged agreement as to the number of bottles. Within the bottle, the milk was separated so that at the very top for about three inches was the cream and below that the skim milk. If the customer wanted the milk homogenized then he or she had to shake it after delivery. If a customer wanted the cream, he or she had to siphon it off. A milkman's job was difficult especially in the winter months. The milk trucks were iced so as to prevent spoilage. Although carried in wire baskets separated for each bottle, the milk bottles were cold when eventually pulled from the basket and set on the door stoop. It was money for Lou and it helped the family. Lou was generous to his brothers and sisters with small gifts as he began to earn a paycheck. His generosity to his two younger brothers resulted in several gifts notably a pair of skis and board games. Lou also became a pool and billiard fanatic much to father's displeasure. For seventeen and eighteen year olds about to enter the service, life had to be lived quickly and the thrills of youth needed to be addressed. For Lou, it was hanging out at a pool hall. "Where have you been?", was my father's ongoing request yet knowing what the response would be. "We stopped to shoot some pool" was the answer on going and continuing. Finally one day in desperation my father said, "Well that's it, I'm going to move your bed to the pool hall and you can sleep there". It was a threat that never saw the light of day.

For Junior and me, Lou was our hero. He was an All-State honorable mention in football and a first string centerfielder for three years on the Crosby High School baseball team. He had many friends both male and female, Lou was a bit over 5'10" tall and a look that the girls called "Tyrone Power".

For Lena (now Mickie), the war had an effect typical of the young women of the day. She was eighteen when she graduated from Crosby High School in 1942. Her male friends were off to war and she like all girls her age felt a grieving that such an overwhelming event can have on those persons who must wait and worry. For her part she adjusted by taking on a task that was her life-time goal. She wanted to become a registered nurse. Thus she applied and immediately entered nursing school at Waterbury Hospital. Her first year was a challenge to find an acceptable relationship and some common ground with the Head of Nursing who also ran the Nursing School. It was to no avail for Mickie. She would come home to report that she could not do anything right in the eyes of the Head Nurse. At the year's end, she passed all her subjects except Chemistry for which she earned a "69" with a "70" as the required mark to pass. It was for Mickie "a predicable end" for the head of nursing was also her chemistry teacher. Mickie was convinced that the "69" was the means to wash her out and thus she left nursing school - angry and upset with a dream lost.

Mickie's headaches which began as a child intensified and she often would cry from the throbbing that a doctor determined to be chronic and migraine. Mickie would often sit in a darkened room to relieve the pain.

She went to work in a factory machining parts for airplanes. She adjusted to a new life with friends on her swing shift. Her hours were from 3:00 p.m. until 11:00 p.m. On one occasion in 1944 when Mickie was now twenty years old, she did not arrive home at approximately 11:30 p.m. time which was her custom as she walked from North Main Street. As was typical, my mother waited up for her until she arrived home. When she did not arrive at the 11:30 time, my mother's pace became more intense. "Where is she? Why isn't she home?" a statement to no one in particular. Then as the time moved to 12:30 a.m., she awoke our father, "Angelo, Lena's not home. Something has happened to her" Again she paced. By this time,

Tessie, Junior, Lou, and I were all up. At 1:00 a.m., Mickie came through the front door. "Where were you? You had us all worried to death." "Several of us stopped for a coke and some had a beer", was her response. That's when my father said, "You have your Mother worried and you were out for beer" and with that he slapped Mickie across the face with his open hand. He had never hit Mickie, Lou, or Tess. It was a moment that stopped in time for me. I can see the scene to this day. My father had such a generated anger that it stopped time. The anger seemed to be based in greatest part upon my mother's legitimate but as it always appeared "unbelievable protective type of worry" where her children were concerned. It was Lou who came to Mickie to console her. They had always had a special bond and at this moment such a relationship was needed.

In 1943, the white penny was distributed. Copper was an important war metal and the white penny was a means of saving precious metal for the war effort. Collecting those pennies became a fad for a while until we decided to spend them.

In January, 1943, General Douglas Mac Arthur moved into New Guinea and captured strategic points of defense. The losses were heavy and gold stars went up in the windows, but the turning point had occurred. The war in the Pacific was also a basis of discussion by the teacher. The discussion focused on an approach by the General that the way to win the war was through the Philippines and then on to Japan. The US Navy however wanted to win the sea battles and take a number of islands as staging areas for the attack on Japan. Somehow both points of view coexisted in this time of need for victories.

One of the most decisive battles occurred at Tarawa where fierce fighting eventually meant the death of thousands of Japanese soldiers. When Tarawa was taken in November, 1943 very few Japanese and Koreans, who were captive workers on the island, were still alive.

In the classroom, we marked on the map and wrote names of places that few if any Americans had ever heard of before the War.

In January, 1943, the Russians had broken the deadlock at Stalingrad. President Roosevelt and Prime Minister Churchill met at Casablanca to demand unconditional surrender of the Axis. It is the first time that the words were used regarding the enemy.

For our part at home, efforts to help the War effort intensified. We collected anything that was of possible re-use. Paper clips, cooking grease, and string were collected to name just a few items. The tenants at 230 Orange Street would throw string on the ledge above the cellar stairs and a job that Junior and I had was to wind it into a ball for delivery to a collection station . The term recycling was far into the future as a term in vogue but recycling was a patriotic duty in the war years.

Saving bonds became the patriotic means to save and to help the War effort. Every few month my mother put aside $18.75 and bought a savings bond. The first one purchased in July, 1942 had a maturity value upon redemption in July, 1952 of $25.00. Beginning with that first purchase, she bought a bond, about each month, until the end of the war. At school there were penny campaigns and dime stamp campaigns. A dime booklet would be issued in a size of about six inches long and three inches wide. The title was "10c Stamp Album". The inscription read "For the purchase of United States War Savings Bonds". At the bottom of the booklet were the words "10c Stamp $25 Bond". Inside was a place to glue a stamp and as the stamps accumulated the total below the stamp gave the new savings amount. When the total reached $18.70 plus a nickel, the owner of the book could trade it in for a $25 United States Bond which would mature in ten years at an annual interest rate of 2.9%. In 1940's terms, it was a good financial deal and the savings helped fund the war effort.

In February, 1943, the British Eighth Army crossed into Tunisia.

In March, 1943, rationing of meats, butter, and cheese began.

In April 1943, the Waterbury Clock Company with plants in both Waterbury and Middlebury subscribed at the 100% level to the payroll deduction plan for the purchase of War Savings bonds. A ceremony was held and the factory proudly flew the Treasury T flag at its Cherry Avenue yard. Congressman Joseph E. Talbot congratulated the workers for their patriotic efforts.

In April, the Orange Street Hobo Jr.'s. joined by a few school friends decided to do something patriotic. "What should we do?" became the question. "We can visit all the mothers with stars in their windows and tell them that we are proud of their son or daughter." "No, that one is scary". "What if we go to a house that has lost a son and the mother starts to cry?" .

A story that circulated in the comic book solidified our decision. The comic book story told of a young teenager who drove recklessly in his hot rod - a car that appeared to be a 1934 roadster. As he drove around town, one of the panels showed older folks "tsk, tsking" and saying, "That hot rod would be the death of him yet". The next panel shows the car eventually being sold for scrap metal and purchased in pre WW II by Japan where a factory turned the scrap metal into bombs. The final panel shows one of the bombs landing on a US Army foxhole in which the teenager is seeking shelter. He is killed. It was circulated throughout the area and probably the nation as a propaganda story and it did have impact.

Thus, by general agreement, the Hobo Jr.'s. decided to hold a scrap metal parade so that we could help provide scrap metal for bombs. As a group, we went to the police station and received a permit to hold the parade. Then we canvassed every backyard and vacant lot for scrap metal, collecting it in a pile over the next two week period. On a given Saturday, we each carried a piece of metal and marched to the recycling scrap collection center. With some carrying old radiators and others pieces of junk cars, we were a proud lot of pre-teens.

In May, 1943, the Allies captured Tunis and Bizerte. In June, Pantelleria, an Italian outpost, fell as the result of heavy air bombings.

On July 1, 1943, the Federal Law which initiated tax withdrawal became law. Before that time, payment was usually made once a year - on March 15th. With the new law, money was withdrawn by the employer and thus taxes due were paid on a pay check by pay check basis. I really did not understand the full impact at the time but I remember distinctly how positive my aunts, uncles, and neighbors reacted regarding the withholding. It was as if the government had given them a convenient way to pay their taxes and provide money for government spending on the war effort.

Sometime during the war years, I can't pin-point exactly when, my aunts were discussing with my mother the new Sears Roebuck policy called "carrying charges". They were extremely positive and happy to be able to buy a needed item on credit. "Sears Roebuck will trust us to pay on a monthly basis and will only charge 9% on the unpaid balance." It was like a gift from the gods. For some reason,

Sears was always referred to as Sears Roebuck and not just Sears alone.

In July, 1943, Allied forces landed in Sicily, Mussolini resigned in favor of Marshall Badoglio. By August, Allied forces completed the conquest of Sicily. In September 1943, Italy surrendered unconditionally. In that same month, the Russians captured Smolensk. The Americans landed on the Italian mainland and pushed through German lines just east of Naples. In October, 1943, Italy declared war on Germany and the Fifth Army took Naples.

One of the heroes of the classroom was General Patton who carried pearl handle pistols in holsters on his sides and wore riding pants rather than a long army type pants. General Patton always seemed to know the way that his Army should move in order to outsmart the Germans. On August 3, 1943, we read that he had slapped a soldier, a private, who was recuperating in an Army hospital in Sicily where Patton was visiting. We were upset and angry. What did the soldier say or do to make Patton so angry that he would slap him? Eisenhower was the next step in the story as we read that he made Patton apologize to the soldier for the slapping incident.

One answer to rationing and shortages were Victory Gardens. On the day that our grade level was to plant its garden, Our class left school walking toward a nearby field. The Victory Garden was a means, teacher said, "to have food in case of an enemy attack or a means to produce food so that the service men and women could have food and not go hungry". We raked, cleaned, dug, and planted our garden on the side of a hill. As time passed, we watched our carrots, lettuce, and tomato plants grow.

Sugar was a scarce commodity as were coffee, tea, butter, milk, and cheese. Oleomargarine became a household word. At first it was sold as bulk lard with a coloring agent which was sprinkled on the lard and mixed by hand. Later the coloring came in a type of capsule that was broken on the lard and mixed. Still later the capsule came within a bag which contained the lard. One broke the capsule and began working the bag with the lard and coloring. Margarine people soon wanted to sell the margarine pre-colored. The fight was on between dairy farmers and oleomargarine manufacturers. Eventually, some degree of reason entered the picture and margarine was allowed to be sold already colored. My guess is that butter folks figured that if you can't beat them join them. Dairy cooperatives bought the margarine manufacturers. or both were bought by someone with an eye to making money. But for several months, nothing could beat the fun of sticking washed hands into a bowl of lard and mixing and mixing until the lard turned yellow.

Another phenomenon of the war years was the sale of a substitute meat product called "Spam". "Spam" was sold in a tin can. It was somewhat fatty in consistency but could be fried, boiled, or baked. It could be used in a sandwich, eaten with fried eggs and/or with fried potatoes. Is was a substitute for meat with a population that hungered for some food of substance, and it fit the bill.

It was a momentous day when FDR ended coffee rationing on July 28, 1943. My mother as was true of the other mothers headed for the corner stores. First, she went to the Russian's and then to the Italian's, as the grocer's were known, with the same question, "When will you be getting some coffee?" "Who knows" was the answer. But within a few months coffee came and somehow the beginning of the end of the war seemed an inch closer.

The cold fall and winter months were a concern. Winter meant surviving through the difficult months with fuel rationing. Heating fuel was in short supply. Days went by when there was no fuel and therefore no heat for the house. When the word spread by radio or by word of mouth that a fueling station had a shipment, the neighborhood headed for the oil yard.

One rather cold day in January 1944, at about 9:00 a.m., I took my sled with our allotted rationing coupons and the money to buy a supply of oil for the stove. On the sled was tied an empty oil bottle. At the yard, the line was long and the day was cold. Over the next several hours, some of the potential buyers dropped out. I waited. As it began to get dark about 4:00 p.m., the oil truck arrived. My turn eventually came and there was still enough fuel to fill the oil bottle. I tied the bottle to the sled and headed about two miles back to our home. It was a feeling of the conquering hero. Mom thanked me and I was satisfied.

There are other "for the war effort" responsibilities that united the people. Automobiles were required to have their headlights taped from the top to one-half way down so that an enemy plane could not spot a city and bomb it. Automobile owners were allocated gasoline coupons depending on one's importance to the war effort. The denominations were A, B, or C with each indicating the amount of gasoline one could buy. Smokers could not light cigarettes out of doors because a match "could be seen from a mile high" or so we were told. In school, we were instructed and tested on identifying the silhouette of enemy planes in case one flew over. We may never have been in actual danger but it was all part of doing our part.

At Walsh Grammar School, all of the students were assembled on the yard for a major ceremony. The school had earned the right to fly the "E" flag for our efficiency for the efficient manner that the school was operated. Civic leaders and such came to tell us how important we were to the war effort.

There were many other reminiscences in those war years. A number of "You should have been there.." types. Mom for instance had me take shoes to the shoemaker to be resoled. She said to tell him that I would wait while they were fixed. He had a sign on his window which said "Shoes repaired while you wait". It was a sign that had obviously been held over from before the war. In any case, I gave him the shoes and told him in my best nine year old voice that I would wait for them. "Yeah, he said, well sit down on that bench because you will be waiting about a week" I walked out - timidly.

About once or twice a year, my Mom and Dad would go to the movies on a Thursday because Thursdays were dish night at the Carroll Theater. Some lucky customer would win a set of dishes. Well, they never won, and Mom would say that she wasn't lucky.

There were treats that were affordable. One or two days a week after school, Mom would sprinkle water and sugar on hard bread that she saved.

A family favorite dessert was "Ice Box Cake". It was made with pudding and graham crackers. In an ice tray, pudding and crackers would be layered several times and then put into the freezer section of the "fridge". In a few hours, we had a torte like cake that was as good as anything that could be bought.

I liked to bake, and several times during the year Mom would let me bake a "Cinderella Cake" from scratch complete with icing. It was fun to do, and no one thought that there was anything strange about it.

In February, 1944, Americans in the Pacific Theater of Operations landed at Kwajalein. Later the air base at Eniwetok was taken. In the same month, an air strike attacked the Marshalls and the Carolines. This attack ended the supply lines for the Japanese. Next came the Marianas, with the objective to capture Guam and Saipan. As each name appeared in the news, we, in the classroom, spelled it correctly and identified its location on a map.

The destruction of the Japanese supply route resulted in a major defeat of the Japanese navy. It virtually ended any possibility that the Japanese could defeat the American fleet in the Philippine Sea. The battle resulted in the destruction of a number of ships of the Japanese fleet including two flattops, a torpedo carrier, and over 350 aircraft.

By early, 1944 Japan was near collapse. US Marines pushed the offensive by invading Iwo Jima and Okinawa. The battles were a last ditch effort by the Japanese and led to thousands of deaths on both sides. It was however a moment of tremendous pride as Americans witnessed by way of the newsreel the raising of the flag on Mt. Suribachi. The impression was vivid and I can recall today the first time that I saw that flag raising in the newsreel.

In early 1944 in the European campaign, the Allies pressed their campaign in Italy. 50,000 troops landed at Anzio but could not move forward and remained on their established beachhead. One of the major fights occurred at Monte Cassino. Eventually Americans broke through and captured Rome on June 4, 1944. The war in Italy was slow and painstaking. A number of students were of Italian descent and were anxious to hear of the capitulation by the Germans in Italy. The allied push as charted on the maps in the classroom ended at Rome in June 1944.

On May 3, 1944, meat rationing ended. "Spam" sales for a time declined.

June 6, 1944 is a vivid remembrance. Teachers suspended any class work so that we could listen to radio reports of the invasion of Europe. During the morning we heard of the thousands of aircraft bombings of the Normandy area. The German resistance was intensive even though we learned that the Germans had expected the landing to be at Pas de Calais. Wave upon wave of soldiers moved to the beach in landing crafts. The eventual numbers were in the millions. Finally on July 9th the Allied forces were able to establish a foothold within France at St. Lo rather than just a wide front on the beaches. We began to follow the battle for Europe. Some of us had brother's or father's in the 9th Army and some in the 3rd Army. We rooted for our brother's or father's army to arrive at some strategic point first.

On June 22, 1944, FDR signed the GI Bill of Rights. My father was apparently pleased by the action. "The government is going to compensate service men and women for fighting for their country." "Is it like money to be paid?", I asked. "No, but men and women after the war can go to school and or get back the opportunities they missed by going into the service." Then he said, "It's the right thing to do.

General George C. Patton remained the hero of the war as his armored US Third Army broke into Brittany and then moved to the Seine to outflank Paris on the south. General Dwight D. Eisenhower, the commander of all forces in the European Theater of Operations, sent the Free French army with Americans into Paris. On August 25, 1944, Paris was recaptured by the French and American troops.

By the end of the year 1944, all three of the oldest Cappella cousins were in the service. Nicholas was a Lieutenant with the Army Air Force. Paul was a Seaman 1st Class in the Navy, and Lucian was a Seaman 2nd Class also in the Navy.

On September 16, 1944, my brother Lou was inducted into the Army. It was three months after graduation from Crosby High School. He had turned 18 in July of 1944. The tale end of a hurricane hit Connecticut that day and winds reached 70 miles per hour with rain extremely heavy. Mom worried that it was an omen.

During those years that Lou was in the service, each of his brothers and sisters and Mom and Dad would write regularly. When he was stationed for training at Camp Blanding in Florida, the letters could be in a regular envelope. Later when he went overseas, the letters were on Vmail.

One particular letter, addressed to Pvt. Louis A. Possemato, #31413835, Co. F 199th Br. 62nd Reg., Camp Blanding, Fla., which was typical, was sent on November 15, 1944. I wrote:

Hi Lou,

How's everything with you all. Boy everything is going terrible for me right now. Mary Sistilli (I don't know how to spell it) is here with Margaret and Theresa and Margaret is driving me nuts. She's the teacher and I'm the pupil. I'm supposed to be studying something but

I'm writing to you instead. Every time I look up she bangs me with the ruler.

Hi Lou again,

How's everything today. Now it's Wednesday night. I had to stop writing last night because I had to study Sir Gallahad and anyway Junior and Dad wrote so you would have gotten three letters instead of two. Ma and I are the only ones home now. Mom is washing the dishes. I just shut off the radio to write again. Did you here the news that tomorrow on the Bing Crosby show Frank Sinatra is going to be on as a GUEST. and then B.C. is going to be on the F.S. show on Wednesday night November 22, 1944. I just poured Mom a cup of coffee and I had a cup too. Jo called today to find out how Lena (or Mickie, her new name) is doing.

Lou I just made up a new slogan. It's "Start your Christmas hinting early!". I just used it on Mom. I hinted for the Electric Football game.

Lou, I am mad that you didn't tell me if you knew a Carlo Idarolla. His family is one of my customers on Beech Street - 152 Beech. He's at the same camp as you in the 199th Bn 62nd Reg. Co. F. Do you know him? BE SURE to tell me.

Pa, Mickie, and Terry went to the Doc's. She has to take a Cyst? bath for 15 minutes - just soak. Junior went to a special scout meeting. I just stained coffee on the other paper. Boy I'm sweating. We won't need a stove in California (the b-e-a-u-t-i-f-u-l) sunny light. Notice beautiful. All our windows will be wide open in the winter. Does that get you mad? My, My, Beautiful California. The telephone just rang. It was Mrs. Brown the one on the corner. She wants her hair done from Dad. Her telephone number is 32681. Now isn't that important? She said that she moved up to Watertown Avenue.

FLASH: Junior and I are going with Cousin Richard Page from Cheshire and Uncle Joe to the Yale Bowl to see Yale vs. North Carolina (?). Isn't that swell? I think that I'm a big shot.

Ma's cooking cabbage and she had an accident. She dropped all of the cabbage on the floor but she's laughing and I have to pick it up. Lou, I have to finish because I won't have anything else to tell you for a couple of years if I keep going. So I'll say so long.

Paulie (PS. Mom wants to read this letter)

In October 1944, the battle of Leyte occurred. Eventually the island fell to the Americans.

During the next several months a number of American victories occurred which removed any control by the Japanese in the Pacific.

In December, 1944, the British 14th Army moved into Burma and met up with American-Chinese forces at the original Burma Road. Chinese Nationalists trained by Americans pushed the Japanese out of China.

In December, 1944, German resistance under General von Runstedt initiated a counter offensive which became known as the Battle of the Bulge. von Runstedt hit the middle of the Allied lines at Ardennes and within a week he had cut deeply into Allied held territory. Eisenhower directed Patton to turn north toward the Bulge. With the assistance of air power the last German major resistance was contained in January 1945. Brother Lou spent three days in a foxhole being shelled and strafed by German fire. As the days went by, the counter-attack became less awesome and his patrol was able to move out and to advance once again.

Later that month, Lou's 35th Division, 137th Regiment captured 50 Germans in a pocket near Recklinghausen. The Germans surrendered stacks of rifles, pistols, and ammunition.

In January, 1945, the Soviets initiated a major eastern offensive on German lines. The Soviets advanced to the Oder.

Patton in the meanwhile raced toward the Rhine and captured the Remagen bridge intact. Allied troops crossed the Rhine. Montgomery now on the north and Patton on the South began the offensive into Germany.

In April, 1945, Russian General Zhukov moved into a final attack on Berlin and encircled the city.

The two pronged attack forced the Germans into surrender in May 1945. While Russians entered Berlin, Allied forces moved into concentration camps and systematically liberated each one. In the classroom, we saw the terrible never to be forgotten pictures of Jews and other Hitler enemies who were released appearing near death from starvation with gaunt eyes and bones visibly pressing against their flesh. It was difficult to hold back the tears as Allies uncovered mass graves where those that were killed or starved to death were buried by the Nazi's.

On April 12, 1945, I was returning home after delivering the newspaper which had as its headline: "Roosevelt Succumbs". It was obvious from the story and pictures that Roosevelt had died in Warm Springs, Georgia. I had to look up the word succumb when I got home. Mom was crying and I asked her why saying, "You and Dad never liked Roosevelt.". "He was the President" is all that she said.

The newspapers began to use the term "last ditch effort" often as it apparently became prominent in the Japanese code of honor. Kamikaze pilots began to commit suicide by diving their planes into strategic American targets. The efforts had a short range effect but did not markedly change the inevitable outcome that was facing the Japanese.

On August 6, 1945, Americans dropped an Atomic Bomb on Hiroshima and on August 9, 1945 American forces bombed Nagasaki. The explosive force of the Atomic Bombs was estimated at greater than 20,000 tons of TNT. The casualties reported were expected to reach several hundred thousand. Among the Hobo Jr.'s, we asked the question whether the American planes should have dropped leaflets first telling the Japanese that the atomic bomb was coming. We were of one voice that the bomb should have been dropped without warning to save American flyers who might have been hurt if the Japanese knew that the raid was coming.

The Japanese surrendered.

For our family, the dropping of the atomic bomb meant that Lou, who was on board ship and expecting to head for the invasion of the Japanese homeland, was saved from such a major and brutal undertaking. He was safe as were millions of other men and women in the armed forces.

During the War years, school children were tremendously patriotic and loyal and that patriotism and loyalty was practiced by adults who were our role models. We were learners as the war unfolded. We worried when the War was in its early stages. Would we be attacked? We said silent prayers in class for brothers, sisters, and fathers in the service. We wrote letters. We cried when notice came that a relative of one of the children in the class was killed in the war. We celebrated when major and systematic victories began to occur. We did not realize it then but in many ways the War years rivaled the Revolutionary War years and the Civil War years as the most momentous and stirring moments in American history. We children were a small but real part of that history.

Chapter Six

School Days in the 1940's

Walsh Grammar School was a three story brick building with a cellar that substituted for a play area when it snowed or rained. The boys' and girls' bathrooms were located there as well. Such a situation meant that on most days the air would smell. In the basement was a room that passed for Industrial Arts. It was a small former boiler room that had a few saw tables and some tools. Grade eight boys were scheduled into Industrial Arts once a week for an hour to make shoe shine boxes or bird houses or some such. This activity was the extent of the experience.

Physical education was scheduled for forty-five minutes three times per week. Usually it was hitting a rubber ball with a bat. Each side consisted of 1/2 the classroom or about fifteen on a side.

Each floor separated the grade levels. Lower grades at the bottom; middle grades in the middle; upper grades on the third floor.

Once a week the coal truck would roll in dumping coal through a chute into a basement bin. It was a weekly activity to watch the coal being dumped. The coal dumping was also a message that the school would be heated for another week. A few times during the war years the school ran short of the fuel requiring all of us for a few days to wear sweaters, jackets, and earmuffs in class.

My greatest fear in Kindergarten and one which I anguished over many times during that year was how will I remember where to sit when I went into the first grade. In Kindergarten, there were the mats and we sat wherever teacher said. But in first grade, I knew that seats were assigned and every day one went to that exact seat. It was an anxiety that had no basis in reality but such fears manifested themselves absurdly throughout my life. As a an example, I have spent countless hours rehearsing my exact words when about to return some purchased but now unwanted item. The more ridiculous the absurdity the more the repressed fear. Yet on major issues throughout my life there was a sense of calm and self-assurance.

By some such statute, grammar school teachers were required to be unmarried in order to teach. Whether that law stretched across Connecticut, I am not sure and I didn't bother to inquire. For us in the classroom it was both a blessing and a curse. Our teachers were dedicated I am sure, but their experiences as related to my way of living were limited and their perspectives were the same.

One such teacher, kept a small bottle of whiskey in her desk drawer and from it she would quietly and unsuspecting that it was noticed pour a small amount into a coffee cup on a regular basis. I would assume that her behavior to some degree related to the frustration and the tedium of the daily task which so many of these unmarried and singularly focused teachers must have faced in their daily lives.

My teachers grades were 1 through 6 were as follows:

- Grade One Miss Scanlon
- Grade Two Miss Wolf
- Grade Three Miss McDonald
- Grade Four Miss Godfrey
- Grade Five Miss Greco
- Grade Six Miss Spellsey and Miss Flynn (Each taught certain subjects).

All the teachers told us of their trips that they had taken before the War and how important it was to travel, meet new people, and learn to eat different types of foods. I had been out side of Waterbury only once to attend the Yale game in New Haven and had been in a restaurant only during the Yale trip. I would not be in a restaurant again until I reached seventeen.

Grammar school became a wondrous place. It was stimulating and exciting and it was almost always physically warm in the winter - no small asset when considering the cold New England winters and the shortage of heating oil or other fuel for home use during the war years.

There were some unwritten rules regarding grammar school. As was true of all the years of my school life, schools were not a place where the sit down toilets were ever used. So I have a record that may be shared with a few males of never having sat on a toilet in any grammar school, junior high school, or high school.

However, the bathroom was the place to which all the boys would run when the school dentist would come to inspect our teeth. How we concluded that all of the years of poor dental habits would be washed away with one rinsing of the mouth, I am not sure. As certain as "he's here", we knew to run to the toilet and rinse and hope that he would not send us to a dentist for repair because my family like other families could not afford the visit.

The dress code of grammar schools in Waterbury consisted of knickers (pants that went to the knees and then held there by an elastic cloth), stockings to the knees, street shoes even when the soles had holes and were covered within by the use of cardboard. Sneakers were never worn because no one would be caught dead in sneakers during school. A white dress shirt and a tie were also required. Walsh Grammar School may have been a public school but that dress code was the rule. In the winter, we would wear a mackinaw, with the additional protection of a sweater. The head was protected by a wool cap with earmuffs. Until one was old enough and more responsible, mittens were pinned to the sleeves of the mackinaw. When May came, the Mac and the sweater were replaced by a sweater only. A ritual of spring was to ask, "Mom, is it warm enough to wear just the sweater?"

School was also the place where the authorities, whoever they were, wanted to give shots, and shots were to be avoided. My Grandmother Mocciola passed this warning down to my mother and to all my mother's sisters. "Schools want to give a disease in order to avoid the disease". That solution to her was shear nonsense and a dangerous practice. So whenever the schools wanted to give a TB shot or some such. I would bring home a paper as did my brothers and sisters and my mother would sign it that she would not permit any of us to receive any prevention shots. Teachers would say that this refusal would keep the classroom from being 100% and I would say yes I know but my mother says no and I can not receive the shot.

Throughout the year the classroom was alive with ideas. Pasting autumn leaves on a window so as to demonstrate the colors of nature was as stimulating as painting a jelly jar and calling it a vase for flowers. The painting of a jelly jar was a particular problem for me with my brothers because in the first grade I decided to paint my jelly jar soon to become a vase the color pink. "Pink!", my brothers said. "Pink is a girl's color!" "Well I am not a girl and I am still going to paint it pink". What I didn't tell them is that pink was my sister Lena's favorite color and I wanted to please her with a gift.

The teacher was the boss and my father made that clear. There was no way in which a report should ever come home of our poor behavior or lack of manners to any authority. Consequently, all of the brothers and sisters were models in behavior. That did not keep me from some flights from perfection.

For one thing I am sure that I was a pain to my older brothers and sisters. As I mentioned, the kitchen floor at home was my desk and I would lie on it to read and to do my homework. My sisters would regularly tease me that I was trying to look up their dresses. Such an interest never crossed my mind but I would defend myself with, "I am not and leave me alone". Their second way of getting to me would be to call me "Honey". "Honey, do this or Honey do that". My reply, "I am not your Honey; My name is Paul! and I'm reading" I must have had an identity crisis early on.

I detested our First Grade classroom readers. They were a bright but somewhat washed out color and were totally unrealistic. I had no such life as depicted in that book. The words were ridiculous and silly. They rhymed and repeated ad nausea. By the time I entered Grade 1, I had been reading the daily newspaper for well over a year and these books were boring. So, when called upon to read, I would read at break neck speed - showing off I am sure. Miss Scanlon would not accept my behavior. Since I caused no harm or disrespect she was a bit baffled. Thus, she decided that I would read to her after school but that I would read while kneeling on the hard wood floor of the classroom. After several such punishments, I conformed and read at a reasonable and acceptable speed.

In first grade, Miss Scanlon decided to use a Robinson Crusoe chart to plot the morning breakfast of each student. About once each week she would have a spot check of what each student ate for breakfast that day. Since I was about three years old, my breakfast consisted of coffee with milk and sugar and a piece of toast. I did not like to eat breakfast and got away with it. Now I faced a dilemma. The teacher told us on a regular basis that eating a healthy breakfast was a most important part of healthy living. The breakfast should consist of milk, juice, cereal, and maybe eggs. What was I to do when she called upon me. Could I say well Miss Scanlon my breakfast consisted of a hot cup of coffee. Would she write a note to my mother and embarrass me and my family? "Paul", said Miss Scanlon, "What did you have for breakfast this morning?" With my white lie, I answered, "I had milk, orange juice, toast, and Wheaties cereal."

"Very good Paul. I will mark that down on your Robinson Crusoe chart". Miss Scanlon wrote on the poster chart, where Friday's feet traveled across the sand, my name, the date, and my healthy breakfast.

My second grade teacher read Dr. Doolittle to us when "the class was very good". As she read I did not want her to stop and had the most pleasant feeling in my stomach as I listened to his exploits with the animals.

During my second grade year, I made a decision that directed my life. It may have been too early to determine such a course of action but once this decision was made there was no turning back. I found such comfort in the classroom that I decided to become a teacher someday. It was in fact a conscious decision made clearly and objectively I thought. In retrospect that decision at age 7 or 8 influenced me for the rest of my life. Whenever any thought of another career entered the picture: "Why don't you become a lawyer?" "Have you thought of newspaper work?" "What about advertising?", I would discount the thought and become more resolute that teaching was for me.

At one time, our second grade teacher decided to ask each of us what we wanted to be when we grew up. Each of us stood and proclaimed our destiny. No one said, "teacher". I feared the repercussion of standing in front of eight year olds and saying "I want to be a schoolteacher". So, I stood, knowing that I would never be a physically big enough person and said, "I want to be a football player". What a lie and a cover up.

I also had too much pride and ego for my age and it took an incident to put some sense into me. Our second grade teacher decided to seat pupils by their report card marks. My marks were second best and so I was seated in the second seat of the first row. I was embarrassed for not having the highest marks yet frankly there was no reason for me to have such scores since I spent a minimum of time on homework and study. But I was smarter than all the rest so I thought. So I complained that the seat was broken. The teacher was sympathetic but said that is where you will sit. I think she had me figured out and I was put in my place.

However, underplaying of ability occurred on a number of occasions. One such occasion occurred in the second grade when the primary teachers decided to have a spelling contest of all the students in all the classes grades 1-3. As it turned out, after an hour or so, I was the last boy standing against about three girls. The word to me was simple enough "automobile" and I knew how to spell it. But I did not want to appear too cocky. I learned my lesson. So I said, "automobile" a-u-t-o-m-o-b and then I paused so as to not sound too sure and said b-i-l-e. Well, my pause gave the impression that I wanted two b's in the word. Wrong said the teacher and I sat down.

Jumbled words was a contest teachers loved to use for spelling improvement with cookie as the reward. A word was flashed in a jumbled spelling. "Hands up if you know the word" My hand would go up consistently. Paul, will you be willing to give up taking a cookie for each of your correct answers. "Yes ma'am".

Snow White was the play to be performed in Grade 2. I played "Doc" and the leading role. I recall the room full of parents watching their son or daughter. My parents did not come to school. It was not something that upset me or scarred me. I knew the rules. School was where one learned. There was no reason for a parent to come to school because that was the domain of the teacher.

My third grade teacher, for some reason, was extremely fond of me. I was the classroom monitor, the class pet, and the errand boy. Each week, I would be given money and asked to walk several blocks to the grocery stores on the corner of Dikeman and Webb Street to buy teacher provisions for the week. I dutifully bought coffee, sugar, milk, cookies, or bread and carried it and the change back to school. There was a real sense of pride in that task. I was alone, on my own, out of school, entrusted, no note, just verbal requests, and a duty to perform.

One day I asked Miss McDonald, whom I remember as being very pretty, whether she wanted to be married. She said what a thing to ask and that she was very happy as a school teacher, but some day she might decide to get married. However for the years that I attended Walsh Grammar School, she did not marry.

In grade three, I was introduced to <u>My Weekly Reader</u>. It became the source of ongoing new and stimulating information throughout grammar school. The first time I heard of the possibility of a St. Lawrence Seaway was in the Reader. The Alkan Highway was discussed as a marvel of engineering and would soon make it possible, the Reader reported, to drive from the State of Washington to Alaska. In addition, an oil pipeline would soon be completed carrying oil from the Alaska territory to the 48 States. Vitamins A, B, C, and D were coming into their own as a new sources to prevent illness and to ensure healthy bodies. Wonder drugs was a term that was coming into the vocabulary. As reported in the Reader, Smokey the Bear made his debut as the symbol of the Forestry Service to build awareness of forest safety and as a reminder that "only you can prevent forest fires". My Weekly Reader was a chief source of new ideas. Whether in science, or inventions, or current events, one could find a readable and succinct report in the Reader. The Weekly Reader predicted that after the War both Alaska and Hawaii would become states in the union.

Miss Godfrey was my fourth grade teacher. I was at the blackboard one day doing long division and I made a mistake on a multiplication to which Miss Godfrey promptly hit me in the back of the head with the result that my head banged against the chalkboard. I changed my answer quickly to the right one and I hoped that no one told my mother or father because I knew I would be in more trouble for needing to be hit by the teacher.

Miss Godfrey loved geography. In addition to all other subjects, we received huge doses of map study. Her favorite words were, "Tell me where the country is located on the world map; what is the climate; what are its chief raw material; and what are the chief products of this country made from its raw materials?"

Despite that momentarily lapse in any type of competence in mathematics, I did learn more about the world from Miss Godfrey than from any other teacher subsequently. Any ability that I have of identifying places on the map, I owe to her and her insistent questions of location, climate, raw material, and product.

Miss Greco, grade five, was a source of pride to the Italian community in Waterbury. She was the first Italian-American female to receive an elementary credential to teach and be hired by Waterbury schools. One time Miss Greco gave an assignment that students were to pick out a masterpiece from the art world and to tell a story about the piece. Who was the painter? Why were the subject(s) chosen? Did the picture tell a story? I chose "Readings From Homer" because it was a picture in our home that had been there long before I was born. I went to the library by the train station and read several reference book reports on the picture. Who was at the chair? Why was the slave there? What was the slave doing in the picture? Were any of the listeners bored? Were the listeners only pretending to be interested for fear of punishment? It was an assignment that fascinated me and gave me a new avenue to gather information - the public library.

Miss Spellsey and Miss Flynn, grade six, taught a split class. Part of the day we had math and science with Miss Spellsey and part of the day we had language arts and social studies with Miss Flynn. Traveling back and forth was stimulating.

I also met my nemesis in grade six in the form of a "held-back" student. He was three years older than the other pupils in the class and had been held back three times. He was larger than all of us and just plain mean. He sat directly behind me. Every day he would clip my ears with his fingers once twice or three times an hour. I would say, "Stop" and he would laugh. I would not tell the teacher. That was the wrong thing to do. My life was hell on a regular basis. Once in a great while he would give me a day off. It was a peaceful moment.

There was also a unique thread that ran through schooling in Waterbury and I have a feeling throughout Connecticut. This thread was a sense of patriotism and pride in one's city, state, and country.

As students in Waterbury schools, we were expected to appreciate the role of our city and state in the history of our country. Connecticut was a major player in the Revolutionary War providing supplies of materials and goods to the Revolutionary Army. General Washington praised the Connecticut Governor for his state's efforts to keep the army in food, arms, and clothing. Israel Putnam and Ethan Allen, Connecticut born, led the Green Mountain boys to the victory at Ticonderoga. Nathan Hale, a schoolteacher claimed by the State, chose to die by hanging at the hands of the British and said these words at his death that all teachers required to be memorized, "I only regret that I have but one life to give for my country!"

Waterbury was the "Brass Center of the World". Within or near the city limits were such major manufacturers as Chase, Brass, and Copper Company, Scovill's Manufacturing, and Naugatuck Rubber,

Waterbury had the Waterbury Watch Company which existed between 1880 and 1898 when it became the New England Watch Company. Ingersoll and Brothers bought the company in 1914 and began to use mass production to make the affordable Ingersoll-

Waterbury watch. In 1921, the Watch Company was acquired by the Waterbury Watch Company because Ingersoll became financially strapped.

In the center of Waterbury were also the location of several historic buildings designed by Cass Gilbert who also designed the Woolworth Building in New York City, its first skyscraper. The Waterbury buildings were the Lincoln House on Field Street, the City Hall, and the Citytrust Bank and its annex.

These facts were typical of the information that was constantly a remembrance in the history lessons of each grade. One was expected to have a sense of pride in the city and the state.

My unwillingness to sing in public relates to one of the traveling music teacher who visited our sixth grade class regularly. When he arrived, we dutifully sang the songs that he would lead. On one occasion he had all the students stop singing and told me to keep singing. When he asked me to stop he said, "Well you are not off key but you make an unusual sound when you sing." That ended any thoughts that I had of singing in any choir.

A story that relates to one of the traveling music teacher occurred a few months later when he gave a friend and me a ride in his car as we were walking home from school. His hand touched my leg and that is when I said to my friend, "This is where we get off and thank you and good-bye". The experience scared me to death.

Like most boys, I had a couple of fights in school. The severity of those fights can be described rather succinctly. Many flailing arms and fists were thrown with no landed punches. Fortunately on each occasions, the janitor was there to save us from any serious embarrassment. "Do you boys want to go to the principal's office?" "No sir" "Then shake hands and get out of here". "Yes sir". And off we went. The janitor was the discipline boss in the school and we knew it. He kept the peace and no one wanted to get on the wrong side of him.

Throughout our school years, public school children who were Catholic were released for religious instructions. Each Tuesday for eight weeks, we would leave school at 1:30 p.m. and walk to Sacred Heart School for our instructions. At the entrance we would have to walk the gauntlet formed by Catholic school children who attended Sacred Heart regularly. They called us two hour Catholics and told us to go back to our own schools and don't dirty our desks. (Or whatever that came to their mind as we passed by).

My connection with Catholic schools and nuns was, in fact, limited. Nuns would keep order whenever we, both from public school and Catholic school, attended the children and youth mass at 9:00 a.m. on Sundays. The nuns would occasionally give a whack with a yard stick if one of us was not kneeling rigidly during the consecration of the host. These experiences were my limited contacts with them - until I took piano lessons. For about two years, I would go to the St. Ann's Convent about twice a month and receive private lessons for $1.00 from a beautiful and young nun who wore the white uniform of her order. Each lesson consisted of the usual practices with left hand and right hand and progressive movement through the piano recital book. One day she asked what I had in my back pocket. "Is it a deck of cards, Paul that you have there?" For some unknown reason I had forgotten to remove the mass missal after last Sunday's mass. "It's my missal, Sister" and out I pulled it. I had never had a missal in my pockets other than on Sunday before and never afterwards. But at that moment all the stars were aligned. This beautiful Sister beamed." Oh Paul I am so proud of you!" "Thank you Sister," was my reply and with such smugness. This moment gave me the courage to ask subsequently about the other nuns in the convent. "Why are they always scrubbing and cleaning?" "Well Paul, it is part of our duty to clean and to work hard and show submission to our Convent Mother" "Oh, then why don't you clean?" "Because Paul, I give lessons on the piano and that is how I show my responsibility to the convent community. Do you understand that?" "Yes ma'am", I said.

On Tuesday, June 22, 1943, a wondrous event occurred. My sister Tess was graduating from the eighth grade at Walsh Grammar School. The wonder was not her graduating since she was always a hard-working and successful student. The wonder was that my mother and father came to school to witness the graduation. I had never seen them at school and the sight was a moment of an indelible imprint.

Chapter Seven

Disasters, Customs, And Sex in the 1940's

The political scene was one aspect of my interest. Another was, without admitting to any morbid obsession, the disasters that occurred in my youth. It is possible that such disasters made me more sensitive as an adult. I would like to think so.

Without trying to develop a chronological listing which can be reviewed in any good reference, my intent is to convey the impact from the perspective of one who as a child and youth was sensitive and aware of the tragedies and who felt their impact. There were two maritime disasters that I recall reading about in the 1940 war years. In February 1942, two US Destroyers ran aground on Newfoundland with a loss of over 200 service personnel. In 1944, three US Destroyers sank in a typhoon in the Philippines with a loss of life set at about 790. In 1944, 322 people were killed when a pair of ammunition ships exploded in port Chicago. It seemed so unfair that men and women would die in what one would think were safe harbors. Such losses profoundly concerned me. I felt that such losses were so unjust.

In July 1945, a US Army B-25, a huge aircraft for the time, struck the Empire State Building killing about a dozen people. That particular tragedy came close to home. New York was not far away and the Empire State Building was constantly in the papers as a reminder of American ingenuity to build higher and better. The disaster became a topic of conversation among friends. We remembered how King Kong climbed the building in the film, but King Long was just a film and this plane disaster was real. "Was the building really that tall that planes could hit it?" "Why didn't they have people watching on the highest floors?" "Why didn't they have some type of warning device?" These questions were a dilemma for me.

The September, 1944 hurricane from South Carolina to New England was not the most deadly but it was remembered as the hurricane that occurred when brother Lou was inducted. Few Waterbury residents could recall a hurricane that came so far north and although the winds at 70 miles per hour were only the last remnants of the storm, it was clear that such a disaster must be devastating to those persons living at the brunt of the winds.

The two most remembered disasters of the 1940's were the Cocoanut Grove fire of November, 1942 in Boston and the Ringing Brothers fire of July 1944 in Hartford.

As it was true of the Empire State Building disaster, the Cocoanut Grove and the Ringing Brothers fires occurred close to Waterbury. The people who died were those persons with whom I could relate because I sensed that I knew them - not as one knows friends but as one whose proximity gives the victims identity.

The Cocoanut Grove was a night club that often appeared in print because it was a focal point for society events. Occasionally the Waterbury Republican and Democrat would carry a story of a debutantes ball or some charity to raise money for the war effort.

On November 28, 1942, a fire broke out in the night club located in the Back Bay district of Boston. When the count of dead was totaled, more than 490 people lost their lives in one tragic evening. One of the sad and frightening aspects of the fire as reported in the paper was the way by which the doors opened and closed. Unfortunately, the doors opened inwardly. Panic bars which opened out and were being installed on newer buildings were not installed at the Cocoanut Grove. As a consequence, trapped diners pressed up against the doors that only opened inwardly and thus the fleeing customers were crushed by the impact of others who pressed against them in a futile attempt to escape.

A newspaper account showed a make shift morgue at a garage-like structure next to the Cocoanut Grove. Bodies were lined up - row after row after row.

One of the diners was the famous cowboy, Buck Jones, who also lost his life a few days later as a result of the fire. As ardent fans, we tried in vain to resurrect the conditions as the fire occurred and to develop a plan for his and other victim's escape. "Why didn't he rope the door and pull it down?" "How could he get a rope around a door?" The wanting to have him and others escape such a disaster was a futile exercise and we were distraught at the loss. Several of us were convinced from stories in the newspaper that Buck Jones died a hero trying to save several victims due to the heroic act of returning to the building to assist in the rescue. Whether the stories were accurate or exaggerated was not as important as the sense that a movie hero could be in fact a real hero.

The Ringling Brothers fire occurred on July 6, 1944. Over 160 people lost their lives trying to escape from the Big Top tent that held the main attractions. We were kids, and kids love the circus. Whenever it came to Waterbury, we tried to find a way to see it even if seeing it meant only watching as the animals paraded from the Waterbury station. A circus fire was difficult to imagine. The circus was fun, laughs, contests, and the Side Show. It could not be a scene of death, and yet in Hartford it became just that - a sad and deadly affair where children and adults died. The Ringling fire stayed with me in my thoughts for many weeks. An article appeared subsequently reporting that Ringling Brothers would never play in Hartford again in honor of those victims of the fire.

"Mom, why should people die in a fire at a circus? "Paulie, what are you asking me? Tragedies happen. Innocent people die."

"But Mom, why didn't some one see that there was a problem and stop a fire from happening?"

"Paulie, have you thought about all of the innocent people who have been saved from some disaster because someone prevented it from occurring. We don't hear about tragedies that are prevented because there is no stories to be written. Maybe the people who are saved from a disaster know about it and talk about it but we don't. I'm sure that people are saved from death a hundred times over every day. So you can't worry about it. Your job is to just be careful." That was my lesson.

Sex was not an open topic in the 1930's or 1940's. It was an era when just saying the word "sex" was not acceptable. In retrospect it is nearly incomprehensible when one compares the openness of today with the degree to which everything that had to do with man and woman was covered up in more ways than the obvious.

It was in Kindergarten that I experienced my first encounter with the forbidden subject. The teacher had each of us draw ourselves on the blackboard. We generally drew with stick figures. One boy decided to be graphic and added a penis to his drawing. The teacher went up to him and said, "What is that?" I wasn't sure if she knew or not. She was an unmarried single woman and the figure was that of a boy with a penis so I was really confused. However, no one in the class laughed.

Once each month, for years, I would be given a note by Tessie or Lena to take to the pharmacist at the corner of East Farm and Orange Street. I would bring the note to him and in turn receive a brown wrapped package of 10 inches by 8 inches and about 3 inches deep. Dutifully I would bring it home. It was not until years later that I learned that I was making the sanitary napkin run and that I was buying a package of Kotex. Such packages were not allowed on the shelf but were kept behind the counter, always wrapped, and sold by the pharmacist.

My mother went into the hospital in 1944. Because Dad was at a barbers' union meeting in another city, Aunt Eva took Junior and me to see her. "What is the matter with Mom?. Is she all right?", we asked, fearing the most terrible of thoughts about her health. "Your mother has female troubles", was the reply. What are female troubles? As we walked apprehensively into the hospital room and hugged Mom, I saw a telegram on the night table and addressed to Albina Possemato at the Waterbury Hospital . It came from Hartford and ended with:

"Love and Regards"

Hubby

Mom had a hysterectomy but that word or what it meant would never be explained to us.

We knew that babies came when a man and a woman had some type of physical contact. In the early years, we weren't sure exactly what that meant but as time went on we became much more sophisticated. "They do it in bed" "What do they do in bed?" "I don't know but I know it is something that makes babies". "Stay away from girls or you might do something that you won't like doing". "Yeah, I am!" As the months and years went by, we became good listeners, observers, and learners. Time and maturity are good teachers.

The movies became one teacher for sex education. Frankly we weren't always sure what the movies taught. A man and a woman kissed and the screen usually went dark. The next scene, it was the next day. A husband and wife slept in twin beds in the movies. My mother and father and all the kids I knew had parents who slept together in one bed. A few movies flirted with sex. In one anti-Nazi movie, a Gestapo said that the female spy would have her clothes removed so as to be searched. The audience booed. My friends and I were ready for this search which obviously did not happen on the screen. They did find, off screen, a secret message which she carried "on her person".

A magazine would not print the word "sex" in its issue. Instead, it began the word with the letter "s" and left two blanks and said that the article would be about certain habits of today's "juvenile delinquents". For a short period of time, I am sure most people thought that the words" juvenile" and "delinquents" went together and were inseparable. In any case, juvenile delinquents, this article reported, were smoking more, drinking more, and having "relations" with the opposite sex more before marriage than in any time in the nation's history. Fortunately, we were only pre-teens during the war so we were a confused but an interested audience.

One day we were walking with friends toward Schneider's Bakery when in front of us we saw what appeared to be an attractive girl. She was wearing slacks something we had never seen before on any woman in Waterbury. So, we whistled a wolf whistle which had become very popular. She turned smiled and said thank you boys. She was not a girl but appeared to be an older woman. Old by our standards but probably not even forty.

I told my mother that night that we saw a woman in slacks like men's pants. I think she said, "Well, shame on her, and then she laughed.

Newspapers, magazines, movies, and radio popularized the importance of smoking in order to be sophisticated. Someone who looked successful appeared in these advertisements. It was an era before television jingles and cute ads but nevertheless, smoking became an American past-time. Many gave in to the pressure. Smoking at school was a rarity but it happened. One might be heading for the "bathrooms' and chance upon some boys who were smoking "Don't you say anything!", they would say. "I won't" was always the innocents reply. One day, as I was heading up the staircase at the end of the hallway at Walsh, my sister Tessie was heading down and her purse fell. She was in the eighth grade and I was in the fourth grade. The contents of her purse opened and out came a pack of cigarettes. She looked at me, and I looked the other way. I did not say a word to anyone.

Tessie was the agreed upon female favorite. Tessie had jet black hair and an excellent complexion. She was fair skinned and attractive. She was much more regal looking than just pretty. It seemed as if she was always in a hurry to grow up. She wanted to work as a young teenager in order to save money for what we weren't sure. She went to work at age thirteen. "So what will you do with all your money?" "Don't worry about it!" was her constant response. Tessie on occasion would buy clothes, cosmetics, or costume jewelry. However, she always seemed to have a reserve of funds. She became the family's non-communicative in the sense that her business was always her business and nobody else's.

She was however a bit of a prude to the extreme. Girls her age had to conform to high moral standards and any one who did not meet those high standards was critiqued with a vengeance.

A small family problem arose regarding her employment at Aunt Phil's and Uncle Jim's Drug and Cigar Store where she worked. Someone had stolen a watch and Aunt Phil questioned Tess. She was devastated that her Aunt would ask her about the disappearance of the watch. It soured the relationship and eventually Tess quit the job. She felt betrayed by flesh and blood.

Pin-ups became the rage for showing "sex". Betty Grable was the pin-up beyond anyone's previous imagination. Her picture, now famous, standing with her back to the camera but turned slightly forward so that all her curves shown was a picture to drool over. Maybe we weren't entirely sure why but it was obvious that this woman was one who had "sex appeal".

However, within the structure of the 1940's there was an inherent innocence that is now difficult to describe given the nation's present degree of tolerance or indifference to sex in all places. Children were innocent. There were no drugs and an open sexual revolution was not in vogue. When Gene Krupa was involved with marijuana it made the headlines. It was discussed and tsched tsched. How could someone become involved in such a terrible thing as drug use. Newspaper articles began to suggest that jazz musicians were susceptible to marijuana use because of the type of music that they play. Addiction to heroin was an unknown quantity but when Barney Ross, a prize fighter and a war time hero became addicted to heroin when being treated for his war wounds, a sympathetic community was concerned and hoped for the best for him.

Standards were imposed without much shouting. Certain rules of civility were in vogue. A boy would rise from his seat on a bus and give it up to any woman standing. Yes, sir and no, sir were used without a hint of discomfort. A butcher who slid his thumb ever so slightly on a scale was publicly chastised by the customers and in a public setting. Business was to be conducted with character and integrity.

When leaving a movie one Saturday, a friend and I were walking in front of the A&P Market slightly down from the Green and across from Immaculate Conception Church. On the sidewalk was a $10 dollar bill. Ten dollars was about one-third of my father's weekly pay in 1944. I picked it up and began my dilemma, but such a concern was short-lived. I went into the A&P and gave the $10 to the store clerk telling him where I found it and giving him my name. It was not my money and someone had lost it. As we walked further, I saw the policeman who usually had a beat in front of the Carroll Theater. I told him what had happened and he walked us back to the A&P to be sure that they had my name and would call me if no one claimed the money.

When I went home I told my folks who looked at each other, shrugged, and said nothing as if it were expected of any of their sons or daughters. I did not receive a notice that the $10 bill would be returned to me.

On several occasions I would come home by way of St. Stansislaus Church and, occasionally, usually on Mondays, I would see a priest get into a late model Cadillac. The Cadillac had a chauffeur with a woman in the back seat where the priest also sat. I told my mother what I saw. For me, it was neither thinkable nor acceptable that in 1940's Waterbury a priest could have a female friend. She said, "Well maybe it was his mother or his sister or his aunt. Priests can have families too." That conversation was the end of my great concern that a priest was in an automobile with a woman. My mother's answer was the important lesson. By that response and others, I, and all the family, were taught a lesson that one should not jump to conclusions and that one should not think the worst at first glance.

There were several aspects to my mother's personality. She was at times prudish, as well as humorous, as well as curious. All these were sides to our mother. On one hand, men in general who chased women were "pigs" and women in general whom the men chased were "loose women". Men might not be trustworthy and if any tired to "get smart with us" we were to kick them in the shins and run. The most risqué behavior she would ever show was to say on occasion, "Ladies and gentlemen take my advice, pull down your pants and slide on the ice", and then she would laugh.

She wanted to be modern to a degree as long as it did not interfere with her inherent sense of morality as passed down through the generations. Virtues were taught by example and by pointing out the lack of virtue in some situation. A person who showed a lack of respect or integrity in some newspaper article or some incident on the street became an example she would use with us of how not to act. Honor was important and "never airing family problems in public" was a rule that must be practiced. Fair play was essential and a sense of humor kept things in perspective even in the most difficult of times. Each of her children must address their better self and not follow the worst example. If we were to be influenced, then let it be the behavior which was uplifting. Bide one's tongue unless the values taught are challenged. She would tell us that the job that she and Dad had were to instill in us character, determination, and persistence. We had the job of practicing these virtues whether Mom and Dad were present or not. We were not necessarily taught to be rugged individuals but we were taught to conform to a higher level. Such a higher level has its rewards when it teaches that as a person you are more important than any frivolous idea or dishonorable action or request to tempt you. Your responsibility was to reject that which was not good for you or not in your best interests.

She was also curious about sports. She loved to hear and read about sport teams and to understand sports expressions that were used. Such curiosity led to good humored disagreements. If Mom asked me what something meant, I would explain it in detail much to her exhaustion and determination to get out from under the question. One of many such discussions involved "round robin" versus "sudden death" tournaments. My persistence to explain by examples until she repeated what I had said would leave to an exasperated mother who would invariably say, "I'm sorry I asked".

The special relationship that I had with my mother while not always a text book example of loving between mother and son was often challenging and humorous. I would say, "Don't put any onions in the salad next time." She would say, "Take them out if you don't like them." I would say. "Why do you put onions in the salad?" She would say, "for flavor." I would say, "then if the flavor is in the salad what good is it to take the onions out?" So it went with our conversations. We would "argue" about countless daily tasks and processes - How to sweep the floor, How to wash a dish, How to dust under the table (a task for me because I was the smallest and the youngest), or How to use the Singer Hand Held Vacuum on the sofa. She kept a sense of humor throughout all such encounters. "Paul, I have a special job for you someday. When they come and get me for doing in my youngest son or for knocking some sense into him because he is a pain in the back side then you better have become a lawyer to defend me for what I have done to you!"

The Catholic faith played a major role in our belief system. Catholic traditions were permeating and dominating in our lives. Movies that were censored and failed to receive the Legion of Decency approval were condemned. Catholics were forbidden from seeing such films. We as a family would never question the rating. If the Legion of Decency said no then it was no. On certain holy days, seven churches had to be visited within which a prayer was to be said for special dispensations. Rosary beads purchased could not be used immediately because no value would come of the prayers that were said using them unless such beads were first blessed by the priest and sprinkled with holy water.

Mass was a weekly responsibility and holy communion was only taken if during the previous week the repentant went to confession. A holdover using one confession to take holy communion several times was not permissible. Catholics would not attend a Protestant church for Sunday services and only with some reluctance into a Protestant church for a marriage ceremony. Such Protestant weddings were a rarity any way since Waterbury was overwhelmingly Catholic or at least our circle of friends was Catholic. Hats or head coverings were always worn by women within church. Meat was never eaten on

Friday - any Friday. Rules that kept us as Catholics in a state of anxiety and conformity were prevalent. Yet the religion remained satisfying and comforting. There was a sense of peace and satisfaction that we had the one true religion or so we were instructed, originated by Jesus, explained by St. Paul, and passed down through Peter and the Popes.

A moral and ethical code continued to exist in the 1940's. Society was straight laced; however, some flexibility in the rigidity was emerging with the changing times. Maybe it was due to young men going off to war that made displays of affection more acceptable and more prevalent in public. Men and women kissed on the street without criticism.

Newspaper and magazine advertisements had much to do with the changes in behavior as did a more permissive approach in the movies. Movies began to show their female stars with a bit less clothing.

Cigarettes were being advertised in the magazines and used in the movies as if they were an important part of social status. Movie stars always seemed to be lighting a cigarette or smoking one.

Men in uniform with great big smiles and well groomed looks advertised that they drank American bourbons.

The changes in behavior did not appear to be offensive to a society that was undergoing the trauma of a war and a need for focused energy that such a trauma dictated.

Chapter Eight

Entertainment

The most powerful influence beyond the home, church, and school was the motion picture. Nothing brought the world as close as the movies and newsreels. Saturday and Sunday were days of experiencing, although vicariously, the world that existed beyond Orange Street, Walsh Grammar School, or Waterbury. Movie stars were glamorous. They lived in world that appeared to be wise, witty, and occupied by talented people who entertained us for just twelve cents. The homes in the movies were usually large, and the furniture was modern with a glossy finish and rounded corners. The homes also had well-kept lawns with a number of trees. Stars walked about their movie homes in silk lounging clothes. None of my friends had such experiences except as they came to us on the movie screen.

Beginning with the late 1930's and into the early 1940's, air conditioning became an important lure that brought in customer to the movie houses. Thus, in the summer, movie theaters advertised with a banner across their marquees that it was "20 Degrees Cooler Inside". The banner was also displayed in the front of a number of other establishments. When the summer temperature in Waterbury approached or exceeded 100 degrees and muggy, 20 degrees cooler was an answer.

On Saturdays, we went to the Carroll Theater because it had a 12 cents admission. On Sundays, we went to the State or Loew's Poli for 15 cents. These movie houses were more expensive because they had the newer films, were more modern, cleaner, and up-to-date. Finding a few pennies to have something to eat while watching the movie was a serious discussion of preferences. Blackjack chewing gum was a favorite of several - not mine. There were also miniature wax coke bottles filled with some sweet liquid. Candy cigarettes may be a moment's fund but they tasted like chalk. On occasion, we would buy wax lips to chew. They cost a penny. A candy bar cost 5 cents except for Peter Paul Mounds which cost 10 cents. However, Mounds had two small bars inside so sometimes two of us would pool our five cents and split the two bars. Mounds were rich tasting and full of coconuts.

On hot summer days when the temperature went over one hundred, we would usually buy a Pepsi Cola from a soda pop machine that dispensed large bottles. Five cents would get us as the jingle went "twice as much for a nickel too". On one occasion, we decided to buy a soft drink that new to the Waterbury area. It had been around for about ten years but was rarely advertised in the city. The drink was "Seven-Up". When we went into the grocery store, the clerk refused to sell "Seven-Up" to us. He said that we were not seven years old yet (We were six years and ten or so months) and that "Seven-Up" was only for those persons who were seven years of age or older because it was meant to be a mixer in liquor. We didn't question him. A few months later when I turned seven, I walked in to the same story and from the same clerk I bought a bottle of "Seven-Up". I must have looked much older.

Along with the newsreel, cartoon, and two movies, the Saturday serial was a highlight. Each week the hero, or the heroine he had to save, was left in some precarious predicament and we had the week to agonize over the plight and any possible means of escape. It might be that the walls in some dark cave were closing in to crush the hero; trains might be approaching with a hero or heroine unable to move off the track; a sawmill blades was about to slice the hero or heroine into two pieces; or a fingertip grasp was all that separated the hero from falling into the great canyon below. We argued over a means of escape for six days until the next Saturday and the moment when one of us could say. "I told you so. I knew that's how he would get out of it!" Johnny Mack Brown was a real life hero and a special favorite because he was once a football star. We knew that he really could do all those hero things that he did.

The newsreel in many ways was a highlight of the afternoon. It was our history and geography lesson on a once or twice a week basis. Newsreels also showed us a world that was described usually by the rich deep voice of Lowell Thomas. Australia, Canada, Mexico, Europe, Russia, and Africa were right before our eyes.

New discoveries were demonstrated in the newsreels. One in particular was a miracle glue. The glue could hold an elephant who was suspended in mid-air. Ropes from a tower were attached to a box. The box was glued to another box. From the second box were ropes attached to a saddle which was straddled around the belly of the elephant. The two parts of a box were glued together by this miracle glue.

The Billy Conn - Joe Louis fight at the Polo Grounds June 18, 1941 was memorable. Joe Louis was young and powerful with a tuff of hair and a devastating hook. Most of my friends and I thought that Billy Conn must have some relationship with Connecticut so we rooted for him. We watched the early rounds and cheered as Conn hit and ran and out-boxed Louis. We were so dismayed when he tried to wade in during the 13th round and trade punches with Louis. Even while knowing the outcome, we hollered at the screen "Don't do it! Get away!" Louis caught Conn with several punches and then he threw that powerful right cross that put Billy on the canvas. Conn looked small compared to Louis. He actually weighed 169 pounds to Louis at 199 pounds and wading in didn't work. We argued that Billy Conn got a bad decision and that the referee should have let him continue. Eventually we conceded that there was only one boxer like Joe Louis and he was both an unbeatable champion and a hero.

During one remembered moment of boyhood, Uncle Joe Pazerras (now Page) invited Junior and me to attend a Yale football game with him and his son, our cousin, Richard.

We drove to New Haven in his automobile. He had saved gasoline coupons from his catering business for this special occasion. We had seats on about the twenty yard line. Yale's star was an all-around player named Kelly who, it seemed, did everything - run, kick, punt, and kick field goals. Yale won 6-0. But the thrill of the day was not over. Uncle Joe took us all to a restaurant. It was the only time that Junior and I were in a restaurant and it would not happen again for me until I reached seventeen. The restaurant was like an inn, typical of Connecticut. We had a waitress. Such an experience was beyond us. We ordered a hamburger and a coke.

For all other times, Saturday heroes performed on the screen - Harmon of Michigan, Kelly of Yale, and Bertelli of Notre Dame were three of the most notable during those years. The 1943 Notre Dame season was a memorable one. Angelo Bertelli won the Heisman Trophy while playing in only six games. He left to join the US Marine Corps and we were convinced that the reason he went into the service was to teach marines how to throw a hand grenade. It's a natural we decided. He could use his throwing ability with a football to teach throwing a grenade at the enemy. The marines were smart to get him was our answer to his leaving college football.

Listening to the Notre Dame versus Great Lakes game in November, 1943 was devastating for Notre Dame fans. Great Lakes upset Notre Dame 19-14. In that same month, on Thanksgiving Day, Wilby High School upset Crosby High School 19-14. Lou played guard on Crosby's team and was touted for All-State. Nothing compensated for the loss to Wilby or the loss by Notre Dame. We decided that it was fate and that two great football teams were hit by some evil eye.

When Yankee Stadium showed up on the screen, it was special for most Waterbury audiences because most folks were Yankee fans although a sprinkling of New York Giants and Boston Red Sox fans were always in the audience. When the Yankees came on the screen, we cheered louder than the Giant or Red Sox fans. Lou Gehrig always seemed to have a slight smile and always seemed to be swinging his bat low against the ground. When any Giant or Red Sox fan showed up, we booed - except for Ted Williams. We couldn't get up the nerve to boo a .400 hitter.

Once a year, the newsreels would highlight the New Year's Bowl games. The one remembered most vividly was the Rose Bowl. We would have heard the game on radio late in the afternoon on New Years' Day. However, seeing, just a few days later in the newsreels, the filled to capacity Rose Bowl, the crowd, the weather, and the typical pre-game views of pretty girls smiling next to orange trees was memorable. Outside of our movie house, it was ten degrees and snowing. In California, on New Years Day, it was 75 to 80 degrees. In the recesses of the mind, I saw myself one day picking an orange from some three thousand mile away orange tree.

Technicolor and a process called sepia became modern innovations. No matter how good or how bad the Technicolor movies may have been, we went as often as possible to see a movie that was in Technicolor. Sepia that brownish film process seemed to disappear as a screen gimmick.

The films of 1939 began a move toward quality that continues today. *Gone with the Wind* was not approved for Catholic viewing so we were not allowed to see it, but we heard about the scene at the staircase. "He said 'damn' in the picture. Wow!"

The *Hunchback of Notre Dame* was fascinating. The scenes within the church and above the church tower added realism to the movie. Charles Laughton was believable as a lonely and taunted misfit. Maureen O'Hara was beautiful.

The *Wizard of Oz* was a fun movie. The lion, scarecrow, and the tin man were memorable characters. The evil witch gave us someone to boo and the munchkins were intriguing because we had never seen so many little people.

Drums along the Mohawk was frightening. If it were history, it certainly was graphic. The scenery and the exploits kept us on the edge of our seats.

Because we knew it was a love story, we reluctantly went to see *Wuthering Heights* . I remember how the hero and heroine were both so romantic and so sad.

Jesse James introduced Tyrone Power and Henry Fonda to me. Both became favorite movie heroes. In later years, the movie *Return of Frank James* was one we had to see because it was a sequel to *Jesse James*. Henry Fonda, as Frank James, was going to avenge the death of his brother Jesse.

The Philadelphia Story was a type of life that we knew nothing about and the story was lost on us. However, from that picture on, I knew that any girl that I would like would have to have slightly cat eyes and a strong jaw with high cheek bones and look a lot like Kathryn Hepburn.

Northwest Passage depicted life among the adventurers who would go into new territories. History films were my favorite. This film with Spencer Tracy and Robert Young was one of the best.

The Grapes of Wrath was a lesson of hardship, family survival, and determination. I remember the simple eloquence of Henry Fonda and a powerful portrayal by Jane Darwell. It seemed that the message was one of hope, but there also was evidence of anger at anyone in authority . It portrayed police as bullies. I wasn't sure if that message was true or not. Were police bullies? Irish police officers were to be avoided in Waterbury but they didn't seem to bother us except for an occasional, "What are you boys doing?" when we may be just standing somewhere. Occasionally, they would run us off the street when we were playing ball.

Citizen Kane was interesting but had too little action for us. Maybe the message was just too mature.

The Maltese Falcon introduced villains with great class in both Sydney Greenstreet and Peter Lorre. My friends and I were not sure whether Humphrey Bogart could or could not act or was so good that he did not have to act.

Sergeant York made us proud to be an American. His simple life with high standards was redefined by a greater cause. Gary Cooper became a hero. I suppose it also prepared Americans to fight a war.

Blood and Sand was a sad picture for me. Tyrone Power is gored in the bullring. Rita Hayworth goes on to another bullfighter. The one who loved him, Linda Darnell, was left with only a broken heart.

One of the most enjoyable movies that I recall about this time was *Ball of Fire.* The advertisements were very suggestive yet the picture was a comedy about seven reclusive professors who learn dancing and hip language from an exotic dancer. The professors were all wonderful in their parts and Stanwyck and Cooper were very effective.

After coming out of the movie house and seeing *Ball of Fire,* we walked past an open produce market. Junior and I had been sent on several occasions to the Day Old Bakery so we knew the price of food. We could spot a good buy on a loaf of bread or a package of crullers. There on display at the produce stand as a special price was a large head of lettuce for 4 cents. I searched in my pocket and mustered up the 4 cents. A deal like this one could not be overlooked.

Sullivan's Travels was a movie that I remember for content and message, The scenes of hobo camps and down and out drifters of the depression remain with me today. The movie is an historical record of a time that was difficult for Americans; yet there was a dignity in a number of scenes. Generosity and caring were prevalent even when many people had nothing. The scene in the chain gang camp as convicts watched a cartoon was poignant.

How Green Was My Valley was educational by showing the life of Welsh miners and their struggle for survival. It starred Walter Pidgeon and Maureen O'Hara. Watching her on the screen was always a treat.

Kings Row described life in a pre-war mid-west town with suggestions of a sordid life style that made most my friends and me a bit uncomfortable. We liked the music and especially a performance by a tragic film character played by Ronald Reagan.

Bambi the story of a deer in the forest was just too sweet for me, but Pinocchio and Snow White and the Seven Dwarfs gave me a warm feeling of enjoyment.

Reap the Wild Wind had a great cast with Ray Milland, Paulette Goddard, John Wayne, Robert Preston, Raymond Massey, Susan Hayward, and Charles Bickford. It was a perfect picture for us. It was in Technicolor. It had a villain we could boo and treacherous underwater scenes that were realistic.

A movie that stayed with me in the same manner as *Sullivan's Travels* was *The Ox-Bow Incident* with Henry Fonda, Dana Andrews, Anthony Quinn, Jane Darwell, and Harry Morgan. The manner in which a lynch mob determines what is justice and the fate of another person was unforgettable. It seemed much more logical to side with the level-headed people. In many ways the movie determined my attitude toward fair play and justice for the rest of my life.

Heaven Can Wait starred Gene Tierney, Don Ameche, Charles Coburn, Laird Cregar, and Spring Byington. I especially liked Don Ameche. The comedy was a fantasy about a person recalling his past and believing that he was a sinner. Gene Tierney was another star who had pretty eyes and high cheekbones and I liked looking at her.

A series of movies about *Tarzan* deserve a special place. Herman Brix, or as he was later called - Bruce Bennett - was an athlete of some accomplishment. We believed he was capable of those athletic stunts. However, there was only one Tarzan to us. It was Johnny Weismuller, who was an Olympic swimming champion in the 100 meters in both 1924 and in 1928 and a 400 meter Olympic champion in 1924. Johnny Weismuller held numerous world swimming records. We believed what was happening on the screen. He could actually swim faster than the crocodiles.

Several movies were sophisticated but still entertaining. They seemed to come in a series. *Gaslight* was a thriller about a man driving his wife crazy. Charles Boyer was the villain and his French accent made him even more believable. Ingrid Bergman and Angela Lansbury also starred. *Arsenic and Old Lace* was a comedy of sorts even though it was about two murderers. We didn't take it seriously and knew it was a play. Cary Grant was enjoyable to watch on the screen because he moved so differently - sort of like a cat. The cast was a good one - including Priscilla Lane, Raymond Massey, Peter

Lorre, James Gleason, whom we always liked in a picture. *Double Indemnity* was as good as it gets. Fred MacMurray was enticed to murder for insurance money by a seductive Barbara Stanwyck. Edgar G. Robinson (who always reminded me of my father) as the insurance investigator wouldn't give up and pursued his friend and colleague MacMurray.

Laura was a classic movie thriller and mystery. It starred Gene Tierney, Dana Andrews, Clifton Webb, and Vincent Price. Dana Andrews falls in love with a picture of Laura and at the same time tries to discover who killed her.

Home In Indiana was entertaining. The movie was about harness racing, something I had never seen before or new very much about. In a different way, it was also educational showing farms, barns, horses, livestock, grass, and scenery which were all beyond my experiences.

There were also a significant number of "war movies". Some were good; some were maudlin; and some were intended to raise patriotic levels. The *Five Sullivan Brothers* was a tear jerker. It wasn't possible to watch the last scene and not feel absolutely wiped out when the younger brother once again calls to his older brothers to wait up for him. Some war movies just didn't make sense. In a movie, I think called *Bataan* or *Back to Bataan,* a marine, manning a machine gun nest in the last scene, is shooting Japanese soldiers as they are charging up the hill. That is the end of the picture. But then a voice, which sounded very much like Cecil B. DeMille, comes over a darkened screen and says that the marine was captured and is now a prisoner. Such an ending did not make sense to me given the number of enemy soldiers he had supposedly shot in the last few minutes of the film. It made the audience feel better, I guess.

Athletics was always our ultimate entertainment. We played at recess; we played after school; we played on weekends; we played in the summer. In the evenings it was "Kick the Can" or Johnny Jump the White Horse" or "Drop the Handkerchief" (that one sounds a bit wimpy). Some times in winter we had an unsuspecting newcomer put his tongue to a telephone pole with the obvious result of it (the tongue) becoming stuck (hot against cold) and his need to pull the tongue off while losing some skin.

Daring feats were a way of life. Brave enough or not, one was obligated to accept a dare. The flats in which many of us lived were above the street level by two sets of stairs. At the second level was a wall with a railing. As a regular test of boyhood, it was necessary not to walk down the stairs but to flip over the rail and land on the sidewalk - hopefully feet first. The feat was executed by running to the railing, laying one's stomach on the railing, hitting the other side of the wall with one's hand, and then flipping over and landing six feet down feet first.

Another dare was the winter run from the icicles which hung precariously dripping and melting from the roofs about twenty-five feet above. As they melted, the icicles crashed to the ground. When the melting process began, it was a dare to run along the walk directly below the awaiting ice daggers without being hit on the head. It was acceptable to look up in order to avoid the impending crash.

"Johnny Jump the White Horse" was a tough game which required one team to attach itself to a telephone poll by way of a leader. The team members would lock themselves by encircling and bending over one after the other tucking their heads to the side. The other team on offense jumped, one at a time, on the backs of the team against the poll in order to break the team down and for the team to crumble in the fewest jumps.

"Drop the Handkerchief" was a game of speed when players formed a large circle and the one who was "it" would drop a handkerchief or some rag behind the back of one of the persons in the circle. He then would have to circle the group and assume the spot of the one who was chasing before being tagged.

"Kick the Can" was a form of baseball except one would kick a can instead of hit a ball. The rest of the game was similar to baseball depending on the number of players.

Roller skates were adjustable for length by a sliding mechanism in the middle and grips on the side which were made to fit by turning a key. The grips held the skates to the shoes. The sidewalks and the streets were bumpy but everyone had to be a skater. It was a rule to live by. Trading skates was part of the process. If one didn't have a pair then he waited for his turn to fit the skates and get a chance.

Because there was no money for a bicycle, Junior and I were concerned as to how we could learn to ride one. Eventually we hit upon the plan to borrow a bike and to learn to ride. But there was no one who had a bike that was willing to lend it to someone who wanted to learn. We asked our friends. Do you know where we can borrow a bike? Eventually we learned that an old bike was stored in a cellar, was not being used, and was long since abandoned. We went to the house. "Can we use it, lady?", was our plea. Out from a neighbors cellar came a green 1920's vintage bike that one of our friends said was used in European racing. It was a rusted shade of green with narrow rims and tires. We oiled it and adjusted the brakes and thus began our quest for competence. First, Junior rode as I ran along side to steady it and then I rode with him along side. Time and falls later, we had conquered the bike riding and set upon the task of peddling up Wood Street.

In the winter, the games changed.

Winter sports could be dangerous but there was a wonderful feeling leaving with brothers and sisters after dinner to head for Fulton Park with a pair of skates over one's shoulder. Skates were inherited from a neighbor or purchased for a dollar from a second hand sale and were shared. Fitting into shoes too big meant stuffing tissue paper in the toes. The air was crisp and one's breath would come out from the throat. Skating ability generally depended on age. The littlest ones were on the edge near the summer time shore. Older ones ventured farther out but not too far because there was always the sign present, "Danger Thin Ice". On a rare occasion there was someone who ventured too far. Out came the ladder and ropes thrown across the safe ice and one brave "skating life guard" had to belly crawl to the adventurous one in peril in order to retrieve him (always a him) from the pond's freezing waters.

Closer to home, sleds were brought out after dinner and the "flyer" would usually be belly flopped down the Orange Street hill. Once down the hill, the sledder would head back up to give the next person a chance for a ride. A dangerous activity was the grabbing on to the bumper of an occasional automobile that came by and with the auto's speed have a faster and more dangerous ride to the bottom.

After a snow fall, we would form blocks of snow and build an igloo fort complete with a roof. To solidify the fort, we poured water slowly over the snow to cause an ice covering to occur. The fort was our headquarters until higher temperatures took their toll.

However, in winter or summer, the ultimate game of choice and satisfaction was baseball. All through the winter, we talked baseball and held discussion on the best of the major league players and the major league teams. Each of us waited for the day that our mother would let us wear only a sweater for warmth instead of a mackinaw because that meant spring was coming and baseball could begin again. Out from under our beds came hardballs wrapped in black tape, tennis balls for practicing throwing curves, bats, and gloves, if we had them. Unbridled enthusiasm also emerged in a manner that was indescribable. It was spring and summer was coming and it was time to set up teams, rework the arm, and get one's eye back.

Whatever equipment that we could muster among the Hobo Jr.'s. was a blessing. Since there were so few gloves, it was always the rule to throw gloves down leaving the field so that the other team members could use them. The leaving of the gloves on the field was in the manner of the major leaguers who would throw their gloves to a favorite spot on the field as described by the baseball radio broadcasters. Sometime later the throwing of gloves by major leaguers stopped as a practice and gloves were carried into the dugout. But because we had so few gloves and other equipment, we had no choice but to continue the practice.

Baseball bats were scarcer than gloves and pity the player who held the bat with the label in the wrong position thereby possibly causing a cracked bat. On an occasion or two when the bat was held in the wrong position and such a terrible event as a cracked bat occurred, the offending player had to take the bat home and have some one, of greater skill, glue it and then nail it together. Once glued and nailed it was taped and hopefully usable again.

In 1944, because he was working two jobs, Dad had enough money to buy a surprise present for Junior and me. One spring day, he came home with a paper bag, gave it to us, and said open it. Inside was a baseball glove, for which he paid $4.75. The glove was in the style of the pre-1940's but it was only type of glove that available during the war shortages. On that day and thereafter, we took turns using the glove and tossing it to our favorite spot on the ground as one of us came in from playing defense.

Playing baseball in Waterbury was hazardous because there were few if any baseball diamonds. Hamilton Park was quite a hike from Orange Street so we walked there only if we were playing in some type of YMCA league. We did walk to the Park once to see the House of David play an exhibition game of baseball. Generally, we walked to the coal fields by St. Mary's Church. The ground was covered with a soft type of coal deposit and when a baseball hit a particularly large piece of coal it meant a bad hop base hit. It was a hazard but the field supplied us with uninterrupted play as distinguished from playing in the street.

During one of those playing days, I was confronted by a rather competent ballplayer named Richard who played baseball on the coal field with us on occasion. He said to me in front of my friends, "You're afraid of the baseball." "I am not", I replied with more sound than commitment. "All right," he said, "I am going to throw the ball at you from here and you are going to catch it". The distance was about fifteen feet. If I protested, I knew that I would be labeled. So I said, "Go ahead throw it." He did and I turned my back on the ball and walked away. I could never have caught the ball at that distance and that speed. So I decided to turn and walk and say nothing. The truth is that the baseball did hurt the bone on my left hand. I was not afraid to hit and would hang in on pitchers despite my difficulty in seeing with my left eye. Strangely I preferred to bat against right handers than left handers. In any case I was a good athlete but not good enough for the sport that I loved best.

One athlete that we began to hear about on the baseball diamonds, as such they were in Waterbury, was a young phenomenon who was about thirteen in 1942. His name was Jimmy Piersall and he was going to attend Leavenworth High School. The word was that he could rundown and catch anything even remotely near him. He was so good as a hitter and a fielder that the prediction was he was going to the big leagues some day.

Baseball kept us going during the war. For so many who had brothers and sisters in the armed services, baseball was a way of keeping the faith in America. We remembered how it was before the war and how we would be privileged to discuss with older brothers now in the service about the best ball players. How good was Joe Gordon or Arky Vaughn? We remembered how we were allowed to sit in with older guys as they listened to the Yankees on the radio. When the war came, we substituted the talks with Vmail. We wrote to our brothers and discussed whether Tucker Stainback was good enough to be allowed to replace DiMaggio in centerfield for the war years.

During those war years, we were content to listen on the radio and watch through the newsreel those players of lesser ability perform while we waited for the war to be over and for the great ones to return. Actually some of the war time ballplayers were good and some continued to play after the war. Prince Hal Newhouser of the Detroit Tigers was an especially gifted pitcher. Still loyalty demanded that we route for the Yankees. It didn't matter that the names of the Yankee players were different. What mattered is that they wore the pinstripes. George "Tucker" Stainback and Snuffy Stirnweiss could be our heroes for awhile.

Some exceptional players led the league in a number of pitching and batting categories. In the American League in 1943, Rudy York of Detroit won the home run title. Nick Etten of the Yankees won it in 1944, and Vern Stephens of St. Louis won the title in 1945. Etten, York, and Stephens also traded off in winning the American League RBI title during those same years. Luke Appling of the Chicago White Sox won the batting title in 1943 - batting .328. In 1944, Lou Boudreau of the Cleveland Indians led the league in batting with a .327 average. Stirnweiss led the American League in 1945 with a .309 batting average - the lowest ever. The National League also featured some good ballplayers. Bill Nicholson of the Chicago Cubs won both the home run title and the RBI titles in 1943 and 1944. In 1945, it was Tommy Holmes of the Boston Braves who won the home run title and Dixie Walker of the Brooklyn Dodgers won the RBI title. Cardinal Stan Musial won the batting title in 1943. Dixie Walker won it in 1944. Phil Cavaretta of the Chicago Cubs won it in 1945.

Several pitchers became well known for their exceptional baseball statistics during the war years. Spurgeon (Spud) Chandler of the Yankees was selected as the most valuable player of 1943 as was Hal Newhouser of Detroit in 1944 and 1945. Dave (Boo) Ferris became a Yankee nemesis and a strong throwing pitcher during the last years of the war and for several years after that. Other pitchers remembered for their good war year records were: Hank Borowy; Claude Passeau; Harry Brecheen; Ernie Bonham; and Dizzy Trout. The concept of a set up man and a closer were not a part of baseball lore for several years to come, but Lefty Joe Page of the Yankees became "the fireman" who was called upon to "put out the fire" of the opposition.

The Yankees played the St. Louis Cardinals in both the 1942 and the 1943 World Series. The Cardinals returned in 1944 and played the St. Louis Browns (the Browns!). In 1945, the Chicago Cubs were having their best year in decades.

An important baseball event occurred for me in the spring of 1945. Tommy Holmes, a Boston Brave with bushy eyebrows, began to appear on the sport pages of the Waterbury newspapers. He was putting together a hitting streak which was gaining national attention. Holmes was the first serious challenge to DiMaggio's hitting streak record. Holmes first milestone was when he reached 25 straight games with at least one hit in each game. Then it was 30. And then it was thirty five games. Was Joe DiMaggio's record in jeopardy? On July 12, 1945, Tommy Holmes hit in his 37th straight game, a National League record. However, Tommy Holmes was unable to keep the streak going and so DiMaggio's record was intact.

Evenings, especially winter evenings when playing outdoors after a certain hour was not practical, was a time for radio programs. Comedians maintained a large audience, Jack Benny, Fred Allen, Fibber McGee and Molly, George Burns and Gracie Allen, and Bob Hope were favorites. In the summer, the comedians had replacements. Jack Paar seemed to be the continuing replacement for Bob Hope. The favorite comedian among our group was Jack Benny because he seemed to always be in some kind of difficulty from which Rochester would save Benny through use of common sense to point out Benny's frailties. Benny's ongoing jokes were always good for laughs. One was by Sheldon Leonard, "Hey, Bud come here". Benny, "Who me?" Leonard, "Yea. you". Another was the train conductor calling out, "Anaheim, Azusa, and Cucamonga". There was the squeaking vault and the "Maxwell" auto which always seemed to wheeze and stutter. It didn't matter how many times we heard the same jokes. They always seemed like fresh material.

Radio family shows were also favorites. The Ozzie Nelson and Harriet Hilliard show featured their sons David and Ricky, portrayed by actors, who both had great lines. There was one Ozzie and Harriet episode when the pet turtle seemed to have died. Ozzie, to make the boys feel better from their grief, described an elaborate funeral that the family would have for the turtle. It worked and the boys were consoled only to discover that the turtle was alive. Then responded with unbelievable honesty, and thinking about the elaborate funeral, the boys said, "maybe we should kill it." By today's standards a bit unpolitical but at that moment it was very funny and obviously only a joke.

There were other comedy and juvenile oriented favorites as well. "Our Miss Brooks" featured Eve Arden and Richard Crenna. Other favorites were "Jack Armstrong, the All-American Boy", "Henry Aldrich", and "Blondie".

On Saturday evenings, Junior and I listened to Bill Stern, a sports story teller. The program began with, "Bill Stern the Colgate Shave Cream Man is on the air; Bill Stern, the Colgate Shave Cream Man with stories rare…", Then Bill Stern would relate some story about sports' personalities. The stories were entertaining but so many seemed implausible. One in particular told of how Bud Abbott and Lou Costello met. They were supposedly on opposite sides in a basketball game and were antagonists, Eventually the two became friends and formed the comedy team. Frankly, it was difficult to believe the story. It sounded so "made-up."

One drama on Sunday evening at about 8:00 p.m. was "One's Man's Family". The chief character was the patriarch of the family who was referred to as father Barber. The other important role was Paul, his son, who lived in the attic and suffered "shell-shock" from W.W.I. Paul was always trying to adjust after his return from the W.W.I even twenty years later. He always seemed to be the sentimental favorite for whom scripts were written. The show opened with a description of the location of the Barber home in California. The home was in view of the (newly built) Golden Gate bridge. It was a sentimental drama that kept the imagination going.

Before school, I often listened to "The Don McNeall Breakfast Club" from Chicago. The cast would sing, "Good Morning breakfast lovers . Good morning to ya. We woke up bright and early just to howdy do ya." Each cast member would be introduced in song. Then each would say hello in song. Trying to remember some of the cast, I recall names like Mary McMann and Jack Owens. One of the early remembrances of the guests on the show was the "Merry Macs" who sang Mare's Eat Oats" (Merrze Dotes?).

During the daytime, I had time to listen to the news and a couple of favorite shows depending on what was interesting at the moment. Listening to the radio at lunch was possible because schools would release students to go home for lunch. Typically heading home meant ensuring that the sole of my shoes did not flap in such a way that my trip home was stalled. Holes in shoes filled with cardboard and soles that flapped were regular occurrences. Shoes wore out. We played in them, went to school in them, and went to church in them. Those one and only pair of shoes was used seven day per week. But I ran home, flopping as I did at times, to catch Kate Smith.

"It's high noon in New York and time for Kate Smith". She would sing her theme song, "When the moon comes over the mountain,..." Then Kate Smith would speak in her deep and rich voice.

Another day time favorite was whether Helen Trent, a poor working girl, could achieve success and stability in the difficult world of work. Helen Trent was one tough cookie.

On certain afternoons, I had to study my catechism for the next week's inquisition. Developing a life long habit, mostly because there was no such thing as a quiet place to study, I studied with noise surrounding me. One such noise was a radio program contest by a radio personality who would solicit votes as to whether Bing Crosby or Frank Sinatra was the better and more popular singer. I listened intently as the votes came during the several weeks that the contest aired. Why I listened and grew concerned I don't know, but I wanted Sinatra to win. Somehow it worked out that both won for different reasons and were accorded high praise as singers with different styles.

One day, while trying to memorize the Apostle's Creed, I heard two good pieces of news about the Sinatra family. One was that Frank and Nancy, his wife, had reconciled after one of their separations. He sang to her, "My Nancy with the Laughing Face". The other event was that Frank Jr. was born. I was really caught up with Frank Sinatra, his family, and his life.

On a rare occasion, a treat came by way of a celebrity who stopped at Waterbury on his or her way to New Haven. Once Willie Pep came to Waterbury to box three rounds of an exhibition match. "Did you know that Willie Pep has had over 250 fights in his career?" "250? that's impossible. No one could fight that many times." "Did you know his name is really Pepperoni like the stick of meat?" "It is not. "Yes, it is." On and on it went. Determining who was right and who was wrong about any sporting event or statistic was an ongoing pastime.

On another occasion, Lena and Tessie saw an advertisement that Allan Jones was coming to Waterbury for one night to sing at the outdoor coal fields which served as the site for circuses, big bands on one night stands, and an occasional boxing exhibition. The Jones concert was free. Allan Jones sang the song "The Donkey Serenade" with an opera style voice. Lena and Tessie wanted to go. Junior and I said that we wanted to go too. Jones was to begin singing at 7:30 p.m. It was too late for Junior and Paulie our sisters protested. But Mom said that Lena and Tessie could go if they took Junior and me. Under protest they agreed. Junior and I stayed out the latest that we had ever been. We actually arrived home after midnight but we saw and heard Allan Jones.

Entertainment was where one could find it. Generally, our entertainment cost very little or no money at all. In a world that centered on the father's weekly pay check and the paying of the essentials with little left over for any thing else, the answer was two-fold: to have friends and to make our own way. It was a wholesome existence with ethical boundaries established as to what we would do and would not do - whether parents were present or not. Although to a great degree, there were always someone's parents watching and any misbehavior got back to the offending child's parents rather quickly.

Chapter Nine

Community and Its Spirit

We waited for the garbage man. He and his partner on the garbage truck came by each Thursday afternoon. Metal garbage cans, hopefully with a lid securely in place, were aligned along Orange Street awaiting the pick-up to put an end to the smell of rotting vegetables, decaying fruits, and coffee grinds.

We knew when he would be turning the corner. He precipitated his coming with whistled tunes which seemed cheerful and usually unending except when he had something to say. He was dressed in light blue bib overalls, work boots, and a denim dress collared shirt. He had an expression that seemed to show a perpetual smile. He would ask about school and wanted to know what had happened during the week. He would on occasion remind us to "mind your manners". His actions were a testimonial to hard work and doing well with that which one did for a living. He never complained about the smell. When a mouse dashed out of a garbage can, he made sure that it never got back toward the flats. When he finished on our street, we stopped following him on the assumption that he had another street and another group to see about its schooling or its manners.

Our landlord was "the big Russian" because that is what he was. His first name was Mike but Mom would say, "go pay the rent to the big Russian" or "maybe we could ask the big Russian for a sink repair" or some such. "The big Russian" never talked to us children. It seemed that with all of our antics we were beyond his understanding. Each spring, as an example, we would build our go cart. A cart consisted of a 2" x 4" board measuring 8 feet in length as the main carriage with two axles which were also 2" x 4" boards measuring 2 feet in length. The rear axle was nailed across the main carriage and had nailed to its underside a rod on which we put wheels taken from some well worn and no longer useful baby carriage. The front axle also had the same type axle and wheels but was held to the main carriage by a carriage bolt with a washer and nut which went through a hole big enough to permit the carriage bolt to swivel thus permitting the go cart to be steered. The front of the go cart was accented by a peach basket into which we put our feet while steering with the ropes attached to the front axle. The rear of the cart was accented by a tomato basket which was fatter and which was nailed to the main axle along with a back support board. One sat on a couple of boards which were nailed sideways to the main axle for some limited comfort.

During the beginning of one spring "the big Russian" began to make some noise on the verandah of his third floor flat. We assumed that he was fixing or building shelves or furniture for his rooms. A few days later he motioned to us to come to the back yard. There on the dirt was a go cart that he had built for us. The surprise was overwhelming. The man never said one word of welcome, good-bye, or whatever, but he built a go cart for us. We thanked him several times. When we took it out to the street we realized that a small problem existed. The front axle was nailed to the main axle making steering impossible. We decided not to say anything to the Russian but to get a hammer and fix it ourselves. He never knew. He was happy and so were we.

Some things are learned by assimilation. In Waterbury of 1930's and 1940's a hierarchy existed. It was explained to me once by my Aunt Phil's husband Jim Tracey. Jim was a successful business man by Waterbury standards. He owned buildings, collected rents from some major tenants, and ran a drug store/cigar shop. He was an Irishman and very proud of it.

The following is his version of the history of Connecticut and particularly Waterbury mores and customs.

You see Paul, the owner of the rules in Connecticut and in Waterbury are the Yankees. They have history on their side. They established the original rules which continue to govern in large part how we act and live. The Yankees still have the big money and they tend to live on the outskirts and in the wealthy sections where we still can't live. The center of the Irish community originally was on Hamilton Avenue near Pine Hill. One of the early Irish families was the Finn's. The first Irish Catholic priest was Reverend Michael O'Neile who arrived in Waterbury in 1847 and lived for a time in the Finn household. The Irish had a tough time breaking through but they did by becoming maids, shop workers, later shop keepers, and finally by gaining control of the police and fire departments and eventually voting into office the city counsel and the mayors that they wanted. Even when an Irishman elected to office becomes a problem, due to some mistake in good judgment, other Irishmen were voted into office.

Someday you Italians may control the city and then you will have those persons you vote into office make mistakes and then you can keep voting another Italian you want into office. Yes, the Italians are at the bottom of the ladder now, but it won't always be like that because some time later when more Negroes and Puerto Ricans come to Waterbury, it will be them at the bottom. But for now and for quite awhile, you Italians are the ones at the bottom of the ladder.

It was a basic and limited but probably fairly accurate perspective on life in Waterbury.

Teachers were generally Irish and Catholic. Police and fire departments were run by the Irish and there were few nationalities other than Irish in uniform. Priests were Irish except for the Italian church where Monsignor Valdambrini was the head of the Italian Catholics. The mayors and city councilmen were Irish and kept getting elected even when scandals occurred. The offenders were replaced by other Irishmen.

Being Italian in Waterbury had its problems for sure. Growing up meant that any number of times when walking home from school or from the store, it was not uncommon for a few guys on the street corner to call us Wops or Guineas or Guineawops. "I hear that your mother has to shave her mustache every day". It was a way of life. You looked their way, said nothing, and moved on.

It is true that the older Italian women seemed to gravitate to a style of dress and demeanor especially those women born in Italy and brought to the United States as brides. They maintained a certain old world dignity and way of life. Generally at a certain age in pre-war Waterbury, they took to wearing black and carrying rosary beads. They fingered the beads with unerring ability to both hold a conversation in Italian and to say the rosary for some previously departed family member. Their hair was pulled back in a severe manner and tied in a type of bun. They sat on the stoop with other women similarly dressed and they talked but it seemed that they always had one eye on the neighborhood. Nothing got by them. Italian women in black were accorded full respect. When passing them on the street, those of my age would slightly incline our heads in a quick gesture of respect and smile. It was our duty to do so.

One such older woman was beyond the age of gathering with her friends. She had apparently become like a little child in some ways. I said to my mother, "Mrs. Sciarra always seems to be lost. I see her wandering in the street. Should I do something?" My mother said,

"The next time you see her and every time you see her you say. "Vuoi venire con me a tu casa?' or "Andiamo al tuo casa subito'. I think that is how it went. A few weeks later Mrs. Sciarra was wandering again, "And I said, "Andiamo al tuo casa". She looked up at me and said, "Si, si". And so I did my good deed on that and several other occasions. I spoke to her in Italian and I led her home.

One Mother's Day Sunday in May 1945, we were playing in the street. Playing in the street was a daily activity. A Waterbury police car drove by and stopped his car in the middle of our "field". Out came the cop. "All right you guys, out of the street. You aren't going to play in the street while this is my beat."

"But we always play here."

"You're not going to any longer".

My mother was watching from the top of the porch. I never saw her move so fast. Down she came - first the five stairs off the verandah and then the eight steps to the street."

"Hey, wait a minute. What do you mean that they aren't going to play on the street any longer?"

"That's what I said lady."

Well, furor is the best way to describe it.

"Oh yes they are. Where do you think they are going to play. Do you see any grass around here? Do you see any playground close by? Where do you expect them to go? Do you seem them harming any one?"

She was really getting started.

The policeman said, "You keep it up and I am going to run you in."

"Go ahead", she said, "because it won't change that they have no place to play and maybe then someone will listen to me".

My father was, by this time in our life, in California getting us ready to be resettled. The prospect of a mother in jail and a father in California was a bit terrifying.

The policeman took a deep breath and said, "It's a good thing that it's Mother's Day" and with that announcement he got in his car and drove off. We continued to play in the street never to be bothered by the Waterbury police again.

The center of the community was the family. Parents took care of their children. Streets after nine o'clock were empty of any one who was not an adult or nearly an adult. There were no street corners on which one could "hang-out". Seniors in high school had some freedom. Mostly that freedom was dictated by the inevitable future that awaited them once graduated. Induction into the armed services followed June graduation ceremonies as sure as there was a class valedictorian. Seniors, therefore, might have the freedom to stay out until 10 p.m. and shoot pool at the local pool hall.

During the war years, it was typical for young women who would have been married by the time they were twenty in prior non-war years to be living at home and working at a defense plant. The 1940's meant swing shift or grave yard shift for some young girls just out of high school. For them social life was writing to one particular boy or writing to several boys if she was not yet been "spoken for". The social life also meant forming friendships with coworkers and adjusting a social life to fit the time one worked. It was a lonely existence for many young women.

Sister Lena said her good-byes to a local boy, Nick, who joined the marines. The day that he left for assignment, after his boot camp was over, he came to our house in his dress uniform. It was a combination of both sadness and patriotic juices flowing. Tessie, Junior, and I stayed in the background as a tearful "take care of yourself" was repeated one more time in one more living room in one more home.

Lena, at age eighteen in 1942, joined the legion of young women who worked, wrote to servicemen, and found friendship with other single and lonely young women waiting for the war to be over and for a boyfriend to come home unharmed. These woman turned the manufacturing industry into a woman dominated arena. They performed tasks that would have been denied them in the past. Lena would come home and declare, "Today on piece work I turned out 82 parts" (of whatever), and with pride, "and everyone of them was approved by quality control!"

Lena was the soft-hearted one of the family. She was the oldest and the kindest. She had a warm smile and soft brown eyes that would melt the observer. She was the peace maker of the family. She was pretty and sweet with an angel like face. She had a strong jaw which came from both Mom and Dad. She was about 5 feet 2 inches tall and weighed about 125 pounds. She was pleasantly rounded with a soft brown color to her hair.

Tess was taller, about 5 feet 7 inches tall and weighed about 120 pounds. She had jet black hair. She was attractive. Boys would write in her year book, "Tessie, Tessie, the American Beauty".

Lou in his pictures looked like Tyrone Power or so his girlfriends would say. He was a bit over 5 feet 10 inches and was muscular like Dad. He had a great smile and was chased by the women. As for Junior and me, who in 1945 could yet tell what we would grow up to look like. It was obvious that Junior would be tall. He had a long torso even at thirteen years. He had eyes that slanted upward slightly. I was small for many years and hardly reached 5 feet by the time I was twelve. But like my brothers, I inherited my Dad's wide shoulders.

Mom knew that Lou would be leaving with graduation. In the meantime, he was playing football and baseball and there was still the need to encourage him and make the best by pushing the fear deep into the back part of the memory.

During the spring of 1945, after my father had left for California and older brother Lou was in the Army, Junior and I tried our best to reduce our output of problems. After all, only mother was there to discipline us. We were not always at our best. One day, Junior did or said something that had Mom come flying after him. She bolted out of the front door, tripped on the threshold, and fell. Mr. Nishibecki was watching from next door. He did not hesitate knowing that Dad was gone. "Junior, you go help your mother, and don't let me see you getting her angry again. You obey her or else. You understand me?" It was expected. He like the other adults took responsibility for the children when it was required.

Chapter Ten

Family and Traditions

Every family has its folklore, stories, triumphs, and disasters. Our family was no different. Most of our stories were tied to the remembrances of my mother. Mom was the perfect daughter to her mother. She was obedient and responsive to her mother's traditions and folklore, however, Mom was also curious about all aspects of life, government, politics, and sports. That curiosity was sometimes a burden due to the tales and superstitions which represented the deep rooted lessons and understandings taught by her mother. She was extremely bright and yet she maintained a naiveté about life that was at times astounding. She loved to listen to the news but was predetermined as to who were the culprits and who were the good guys. Her moral compass was unfailing. She had stories to tell and we, as her children, loved to hear the tales. One of our tricks was to start her talking about her youth and the years before she met my father.

The stories kept family traditions and memories alive.

She was born in Jersey City, New Jersey, she would tell us, delivered by a mid-wife. She lived in Philadelphia as a little girl and remembered leaving her house and crossing the street to visit the Liberty Bell where it was permanently on display. Her family then moved to the Bowery in New York where she went to school. She and her girl friends played on the stoops of the city. She was a "champion" jacks player. One day a horse pulling a trolley got loose, went loco, and headed for her and her friend. The horse bit the finger of her friend's hand. For that reason, she would tell us is why she is deadly afraid of horses. Of course, she had so many fears that it is hard to remember all of the circumstances surrounding the roots of each one.

She attended one of the Children's Aid Society Schools often referred to as the "Penny Soup Schools" of the city. Each day the pupils would bring a penny to school and for that they would receive a lunch of soup and bread - thus the name "Penny Soup Schools". The schools took numerous field trips to acquaint the children with the arts and cultural events available in New York. In the summer, the patrons of the school would sponsor a two-week summer camp for the students. She was an excellent pupil. The teacher would have her stay after school and teach her to bake and to cook from recipes. One of her prize possessions was a hand-written book of recipes written by the teacher. She also helped clean the school house which was one of the teacher's duties in order to be paid.

"The teacher had to clean her own classroom?", we asked conveying a disbelief that such a burden was a teacher's task.

"Yes, she had to clean her classroom, but she had to do more than that. Across the street was an apartment owned by the school. The apartment had a kitchen with a pot bellied stove for heating and a large black iron stove for cooking. It had a sink, a washer-ringer for cleaning clothes, and a foot pedal sewing machine. The teacher had to put wood in the stove for heating and keep the apartment and the kitchen clean. All of those tasks were her responsibility. The apartment is where she taught us to cook, bake, sew, clean a bathroom, and wash clothes. We learned more than just reading, English, science and history at school. We learned a great deal from that one teacher. She became my friend and I was only 10 or 12 years old."

"Did the same teacher teach all the grades?"

"Yes."

"Were you ever bad at school?"

"I was always obedient in school. But once two of my boy cousins who attended the same school were teasing me. I told them to stop talking to me. The teacher only heard me. She made me stand on my desk for an hour as punishment."

Her father moved to Waterbury in 1913. By that time, she had graduated from Grade Eight. Her father, as he did with all of his five girls, made them quit school at the end of that grade and go to work. He also required that they turn over their pay checks to him from which they received an allowance. After one or two years of this treatment, the three oldest sisters rebelled and refused as a group to give him their paycheck. Rather, they told him, they would pay for their room and board and keep the remainder. It was a small revolution with a happy ending.

The way to keep Mom talking, usually on days too cold or too rainy to go outside, was to ask questions. "How did you find a way to go back to school if Grandpa made you work?"

The story continued. She was determined to graduate from high school so while working at the Waterbury Clock Company, she enrolled in Wilby Adult School and graduated at nineteen with a background in commercial skills. She continued to work at the Clock Shop and had many men who liked her. One would constantly stare at her. Her foreman regularly asked her out but she thought that would not be right to go out with her boss. She actually was shy and would not date. One man in particular, a Swede, was over 6 feet 2 inches tall and constantly pursued her. She, at nineteen, rather old to be single in those days, went out with him on two or three dates but finally refused any more requests.

Lena and Tess liked the stories of how Mom and Dad met. Their questions went in that direction.

If Mom was in the mood to answer, she would tell us, as the story unfolded over the years, a little bit more each time. Her friend, Louise Rosa, decided to help out the situation. "She would say to me, Al, you are too pretty not to be dating someone. You have got to meet some nice Italian man. My boyfriend knows several men who are single. One is a barber, works for the union, and is a veteran. He is handsome. He'll be at the wedding we're attending Saturday. I want to introduce him to you. You'll like him. At the wedding, Mom would relate, he kept staring at me. He asked me out and I said no. She was determined not to go out with him. He was a good-looking man she decided but he was too short. He could not be taller than 5 foot 5 inches and at twenty-six he was balding. He pursued. He came to the bank where I was now working. He asked me out again. I said no. Several letters, notes, and flowers kept coming. Louise Rosa asked if I would at least go on a double date to the fair that had come to Waterbury. I said yes. Your Dad and I went on carnival rides and were stuck on the Ferris Wheel because of a mechanical failure. He asked me to go out with him again. His gentlemanly manner won me over. I said yes. We went to church on our second date. I was a member of the "Children of Mary". After church, we stopped to have coffee and my purse was stolen. The next day, a beautiful new purse was delivered to me at work as a gift from him. He was so thoughtful and kind. In 1921, we became engaged. Like all engaged couples we took walks together so as to let the neighbors know that we were going to be married and to let them look him over. We walked in and around Maple Street. We were evaluated by the older Italian ladies in the neighborhood. They were the keepers of the morals among the young Italian couples, or so they determined. We were evaluated by them. The observers were dressed in black with their hair pulled back with buns either down by their neck or up on top of their heads. As they watched and assessed, they would decide if we were built well enough to have children. "Too skinny, too small in the hips. Ah, this one will have many children." In 1923, we married.

Dad, on the other hand, was less prone to conversations about his youth. We knew that he loved sports and he would talk with us mostly about baseball. We knew that he was committed to the barbers' union and to veteran's rights. He also would teach all of us to play card games. Pinochle was a family tradition - played on winter nights and always on holidays. On occasions, the family would play poker with toothpicks as the bets. Dad and I found a game of common interest. He taught me to play "High, Low Jack, Game." When his friends might need a partner to play the game that so few played, I would be allowed to sit in.

The closest we got to a story was the one he told only once or twice in response to how he lost his hair. "Dad, how come you don't have any hair on top of your head?" "You want to know the story?", he would look at us and give us the slightest grin. "Well I'll tell you but it might frighten you. I was in France looking over a trench to see where the Germans were. All of a sudden bullets kept coming over my head, I ducked, but bullet after bullet came whizzing over my head. Each bullet came closer and closer." "But Dad, wouldn't one bullet make just a crease in your hair and not take it all off?" "Who said it was just one bullet that took off my hair?"

Many of our traditions center around the holidays with Christmas being the day that gives us most of our lifetime stories.

Holidays continued as best they could during the war years. Aunt Eva and Aunt Helen would come over Christmas Eve for a small dinner of spaghetti that was served with olive oil and anchovies. Usually that was the meal except for a serving of salad and bread.

The family would sit around in a circle in the kitchen. The floor was covered with a worn- through linoleum but we were together. It was family. We would exchange whatever presents that there were. The presents were practical - socks, underwear, hair ribbons. Aunt Eva would always guess before each gift was opened, and she always seemed to guess correctly.

Aunt Helen would laugh at something that was said that struck her as funny and she would stomp her feet as she laughed. It was a trademark of sorts and with typical childish humor we would later repeat the gesture.

Each Christmas season, the newspapers began to carry rotogravure inserts in vivid color showing the gifts that were available for the coming season. Each year an erector set for $10 would be the Christmas present which was most prominently displayed. Each year Junior and I would look yet knowing that such a prize was beyond any possibility. But the thrill of looking and imagining never grew old. One year the rotogravure advertised a watch with dials covered with a metal that glowed green in the dark. It was made in Los Angeles, California. It seemed like a practical gift that one could use even on the darkest nights. We never had one but the idea of technology taking over the world as the "Join Technocracy" people wanted was becoming more and more a reality.

By 1943 there were a few extra dollars for presents although there still was no tree or decorations. The aunts would continue to exchange small gifts - socks, stockings, sweaters, scarves, and such. Aunt Eva would continue to take the responsibility of guessing what was in each package before it was opened.

Mom and Dad began to buy each one in the family some type of present. For Junior and me it was a game that we could play together. *"Baseball"* was one game that we were given which used knobs and a screen manipulated manually to conceal the pitches to be thrown at the opponent with a spinning dial to determine whether the pitch produced a hit, the type of hit, a strike, a ball, or a ground out or fly out. The game was still using terms like inshoot and outshoot as pitch descriptions instead of curve or hook. The term slider and fork ball were years into the future. It didn't matter. We played the game and loved it. It also taught us a little bit of the history of the game through the old time baseball terms.

In 1943, Lou was working and bought presents for each of his brothers and sisters. For me, it was the small pair of skis which I used immediately on the hill behind our flat.

It was also in 1943, that I saved 25 cents to buy presents for my sisters. I completed my first Christmas shopping spree by buying and wrapping two berets - one for each sister.

The tradition of holiday dinners began to emerge during the last part of the war years. Christmas Eve was the night to open presents and to attend midnight mass, but Christmas Day 1944 was the beginning of a tradition of celebrating in a manner that we could not afford in the past. As time went on, the dinners became more and more festive, but our 1944 Christmas meal was the first in a tradition that continued for decades. Mom wanted this one to be special and a means to keep spirits high. With Lou away, it was the first time that her family would not be together on Christmas.

Mom decided that the 1944 Christmas should have decorations in order to keep our hopes up for Lou's safe-keeping. She decided that we would have a Christmas tree with lights and tinsel and trimmings. Out of stored boxes came some Christmas lights and decorations. My sisters said that when they were younger we had a tree. I didn't remember one.

It was the 1944 Christmas that I displayed a generosity which I attribute to the examples of my father. The belief in giving as a way of life began in our formative years and stayed with all of the family members all of our lives. I had begun to save money each week from my paper route determined that in the 1944 Christmas I would be able to buy Christmas presents for my mother, father, sisters, and brothers.

Mom decided that I should be the one to pick out the Christmas tree. She gave me $5.00 for the purchase. "Pick out a pretty tree, Paulie, and make sure that it is straight" was my mother's directions. I went to the corner of East Farm and North Main to the grocery store that was selling freshly cut Christmas trees. Unfortunately, I fell in love with a tree that was about eight feet high and straight as one could measure. The price tag said $8.00. "How much will you sell me that tree for?", I said. "$8.00", he said, "just like it says" "I've only got $5.00". "$8.00", he said. So out of my pockets on the left side, I pulled out three more dollars that I had saved and gave the man $8.00. I pulled the tree through a falling light snow to our house. My mother loved the tree. "How much did it cost", she asked. "$5.00", I said. It was a white lie but worth it I decided.

On the day before Christmas, Mom sent me to pick up five dozen freshly made Ravioli at a small store that specialized in the home made type. It was located on South Elm just perpendicular to Crosby High School. On Christmas morning, the turkey was put into the oven at 5:00 a. m. The 20 pound turkey would be ready in about six and 1/2 hours. Dinner was set for around one o'clock. It began with the ravioli, then turkey, sweet potatoes, stuffing, fried cauliflower, melanzana parmigiano, and a salad served at the end of the main meal and before dessert . Dessert included fruit cake which my mother made around the first of November. It was kept in a cheese cloth and daily saturated with rum or brandy. Mom served ricotta pie with the fruit cake.

Dad had wine at the table and fruit-especially figs-and nuts. The challenge was to make a fig sandwich with the most nuts wrapped inside the fig. For Tessie, it was time to coax Dad into giving her a glass of wine. He would always oblige with a glass of wine with water added. It was their special relationship and for the rest of us it was anticipated and expected.

That first Christmas that brother Lou was away, the family was determined that he would receive two to three letters each week from each of us during the Christmas season in order to keep his morale high. He was in Brussels with the 35th Infantry Division. One letter received from Lou talked of the pride in the ranks because it was the unit in which Vice-President Truman served as a Captain during W.W.I.

It was also during the 1944 - 45 years that Sunday dinners began to take on a more festive meal. With both Mom and Dad working, and he with two jobs, money was available for a few extras. Sunday dinner had always been a time for the family to gather together and to eat and talk. It was not necessary to require that each of the family would be present because all of us would be present. That's the way that it was. Dinner began at 1:00 p.m. Meat or chicken, some type of macaroni, salad, bread, and some type of home made dessert was the typical menu.

In our family, as was the custom in many Italian families, pasta was always called macaroni and never pasta. To differentiate, we would call the macaroni by its name i.e. spaghetti, rigatoni, radiatori, noodles, etc. The word gravy for macaroni sauce was also common usage. Gravy meant some kind of tomato sauce with or without meat, pork, meatballs etc.

Mom had an ability to overcook her roast which was the usual meat. "Meat should be eaten well done", she would say, "that way none of you will get sick from some germ inside the meat". So we ate all of our meat very brown and chewy. Some type of macaroni was on the Sunday menu and in a red meat sauce. Many times on Sunday, Dad would make the gravy and the meatballs. His meatballs were larger and moister. Insalata verde was usually made with a wine and vinegar dressing.

One could set the remaining days of the week by our family menu. Monday was leftovers and greens - usually a spinachi or indivia or a minestra. The word for leftovers was ciambotta because everything was thrown together but I am not sure that it has any correct usage. Tuesday was fish day. Wednesday was a soup day made with pasta and beans - pasta y fagiolo. We pronounced it pasta fazool. Thursday was always spaghetti night. Friday was meatless in keeping with the rules of the Church of no meat eating on Friday. We would have a frittata made with fried peppers and cheese usually provolone. Saturday was fried sausages or hot dogs cut up into little pieces with fried potatoes. All meals were served with a salad and vegetable. Meals were also served with bread because it was important to butter a slice of bread "imburrare" (when we said it the word came out "inbunne").and then to dunk the buttered bread (inzuppare) into the gravy or the olive oil.

Retirement was associated with the china closet. When we moved to Orange Street, Mom put all her best linens, flatware, and any silver pieces in the bottom two drawers of the china closet. On a rare occasion when she bought some type of household treasure, she would say that it was going into the bottom drawer for their retirement. Thus over the years, retirement became synonymous with saving - not saving money but saving treasures that had no value except in their potential for a life of leisure surrounded by the things of a good life as she perceived it. Ironically the days to celebrate together the use of these material things never came.

It may not have been a tradition in the normal sense but Mom was in many ways the greatest contributor to family lore. If things were not going well, Mom had a remarkable ability to call upon the saints in Italian with the best of them. She would call out to the saints such as Santo Rocco and San Antonio. These two saints were expected to hear her because her voice was loud and clear as she called out in Italian, "Santo Rocco, what do you want from me? Why do we have no luck? What have I done wrong? Where is the justice?" At times it was directed at Junior and me, "San Antonio, what have I done to deserve this behavior from them? Why don't they listen? Please, get the devil out of them!"

Family was extended to mean both within the immediate family and anyone in need. Thus if there was dinner and an aunt and uncle came by they were expected to eat with us. If a guest arrived unexpectantly, then peppers would be fried as a snack to tide them over. If a family member was in a financial bind, Dad was ready to provide help even if it meant his own family had to cut back.

In the early days of raising his brothers and sisters, Dad in many ways became the head of the household - even though he was married with his own family. His brother Dominic was a headstrong man who was also tall and strongly built. In his youth, he was a bit of a terror and was placed in a home for boys. Dad became the advisor and counselor to whom the authorities released and entrusted the younger brother to his care and rearing. With a strong will imposed, Dominic was expected to straighten up, learn a trade, and go to work under the watchful of eye of his older brother. The formula worked. Dominic went to trade school and learned to become an auto mechanic. The responsibility that my father undertook was never voiced by him. He was an example for us and other friends and family who extolled my father's virtue and then praised Dominic for his determination to become a good citizen and not to sully the family name.

A more basic example of the extended family with reasonable limits related to our cousin Beverly who was the daughter of my Dad's sister Anna. Beverly needed a place to come to during school lunch. When Junior and I came home at lunch time from school, we were given the assignment of taking care of Beverly who was about four years younger than I. Mom was working and no one else came home for lunch. Each day, Junior and I would make lunch for the three of us. Sometimes a sandwich; sometimes soup, and many times lunch was an egg omelet. Beverly decided that she had enough of egg omelets and so she told her mother that she was not coming to our house any more for lunch. I am tired of eggs was her complaint. Aunt Anna came to my Mom to tell her of her complaint. "Anna, you are welcome to what we have but it is only what we have. Beverly eats whatever is fixed or nothing"- end of complaint

Family traditions and values also included a sense of duty. That point of view was more noticeable in the direction and the example the family was provided when it came to a work ethic. If any one of us took on a job we were expected to give the job our full effort. Thus my mother, who was on piece work at the Waterbury Clock Shop, would come home and report that she had established her own personal record for bomb sights completed. Piece work meant that she was paid by her productivity with so much earned for each piece made, but it was more than that incentive which drove her to perform. She expected it of herself and by example hard work was expected of us.

There were idiosyncrasies. Most of them -maybe all of them- a result of my mother's strong commitment to her mother and her mother's wisdom or tales of how things should be done.

Olive oil was good for many things. Warm olive oil on a cotton swab placed in the ear was the remedy if there was an earache. Olive oil as a food was the cure for many ills including constipation or upset stomach. Tea was a solution also for many ills. Chamomile tea stopped all types of suffering including cramps, constipation, and headaches.

Arms should be raised high if "choking" on a piece of bread or some such morsel and mother would blow into the ear to put wind in the throat so as to clear the pipeline.

Mom feared "choking". If any one of us coughed at the dinner table and it appeared that such a cough was due to something caught in our windpipe, she would spring into action. "Quick raise your arms and she would blow into the ear of the cougher." Whether it was fear of the ear blowing or the value or the cure itself, the cure usually worked.

She would tell us, on many occasions, in order to reinforce the value of some cure, how, when he was a small boy, she saved Lou from choking when he swallowed a piece of ice. She had him drink very warm tea (naturally) and she blew in his ear. The tea melted the ice and the blowing in the ear gave him his breath back.

Use of any x-ray to cure such ailments as tonsils or sore throat was dangerous. Any type of shot for curing illnesses was to be avoided. Only if the law required such an immunization for enrolling in school would such a shot be permitted, and always under protest.

Anything that was not natural should be avoided and kept from the body. Natural foods and natural cures were passed down from mother to daughter and my mother was a good daughter.

Mattresses should be aired out every day. They were to be folded in half (they could be) and moved on the bed in various positions during the days so that the underside could receive the fresh air that came through an open window. Beds were made up with covers on special occasions when company would come. Otherwise, each night the mattress was returned to their natural position and the sheets and blankets returned to their places for sleeping purposes.

Minestra was only second to macaroni in its value for good health, good muscles, and a good constitution.

Nothing should be cooked from a can because such a food could be poisonous. Salad should be eaten at the end of the meal to help digestion. Milk and gravy (red sauce) if eaten together or right after each other were potentially poisonous to the system.

Meat was always cooked well done. Very few foods should be fried; however, fried potatoes on Saturday night could be an exception.

Fresh fruit was the best dessert - especially figs and plums.

Italian cold cuts should be the only type of cold cuts to be eaten. American cold cuts, because they were made with the by-products of the animal especially its brains and intestines, were to be avoided.

Prosciutto was a delicacy and should be enjoyed on special occasions.

Bourbons, gin, and vodka (a drink coming into its own according to the advertisements of the day) were not kept in the house. Beer was also not necessary or kept. Wine on special occasions was acceptable. A liqueur such as apricot or raspberry brandy could be on hand and served in a small stemmed liqueur glass only to company and only on special occasions.

Certain types of humor were not acceptable because they showed that such humor was degrading to people as human beings. Slapstick comics were the chief offenders. Charlie Chaplin, Joe E. Brown, The Three Stooges, etc. were to be avoided and movie money should not be spent on watching these types of movie stars. The idea that someone took pratfalls, threw pies at each other, and slapped each other did not make sense to my mother and therefore that type of behavior was unacceptable and was demeaning to those persons who participated and those persons who watched.

Within the Italian culture, there existed a humor of words, however, that all Italian friends understood.

A stunod or stunato was a person who was out of his or her mind. He or she was flat or out of tune not in terms of singing but in terms of his or her demeanor.

A gabbadotz or capo tosta was a hard head who would not listen to reason.

Moosha moosh came from muscia muscia which meant a person who was slow about getting something done.

A gedrool or cetriolo was a big cucumber head. He or she wasn't very bright. The word gedrool was like a port manteau combining cetriolo with citrullaggine which means stupid.

Umbriag or umbriago meant a drunk. Correctly, it is ubriaco.

Cornuto was a man who had been betrayed by a woman.

Coogootz is a term of endearment reserved for children or some one who is loved as one would love a member of the family. A mother-in-law might use it with a daughter-in- law. The term comes from the word Courgettes which means zucchini.

Schiffooz was correctly schifare which is to spurn or to be disgusted or repulsed with something especially food served because one does not trust the food to be clean.

A la mozzen is the beggings or the last of the food on the serving plate. It is begging to be eaten. The correct word is elemosinare.

Words were played with in combination with other words to make the language and the communication more colorful.

A number of Italian sayings were a part of the learning process. Dad, whose Italian was scholarly, was disposed at times to deliver a message in the native language. It was intended as a learning experience.

"Chi pratica con lo zoppo impara a zoppicare". Translation: You are known by the company you keep.

"Chi vuole va e chi non vuole manda." Translation: If you want something done well, do it yourself." He would emphasize that expression by one of his favorites in English, "I could have done that." "This particular expression was a sign of displeasure at any one of his children completing a task, of any sort, without doing his or her best.

These words or expressions were not taught as a singular moment as a lesson, but they was understood. Italians were not better than anyone but it would be difficult to find any culture that matched it. The greatest singers both classical and popular were Italian. Many movie stars were Italian. Many baseball players, boxers, basketball players, jockeys. football players were Italian. The great artists of history were Italian. Many of the great musicians and composers of history were Italian. Many of the greatest explorers were Italian. Many great poets and scholars were Italian. The great chefs and the best cooking was Italian. Romans built bridges, roads, waterways, and great cities. The Pope and most of the cardinal were Italian. It was a lesson taught over the years as part of conversations over dinner tables, while playing pinochle, or while sitting at an Italian-American picnic. Be proud to be of Italian heritage.

Chapter Eleven

Coming to California

It was in the summer of 1944 that Mom and Dad decided that the move to California was to occur within a year. The following twelve months became a time for preparation including telling friends and family, deciding the best means to accomplish the transition, and organizing the logistics of selling off unneeded furniture and belongings.

For Mickie, now just a month shy of twenty-one, it became a romantic trauma. "Mom, why are you doing this to me? You don't want me to marry Nick. That's it isn't it? If we move, you know that will solve it." Nick was in the marines and had a major crush on Mickie who, while he was around, treated him with indifference but given the prospect of a life without a boyfriend decided that Mom and Dad had conceived some sinister plot. The crying began.

For Tessie, it was social trauma. She had just entered her sophomore year and learned all the cheers as a new sophomore cheerleader at Crosby High School. "You are taking me out of high school. How will I make friends in a new school - in California! I have friends at Crosby. I'm popular." Tessie was not the crying type but still was devastated.

For Junior and for me, California was like the promised land. We boasted to our friends. We will live where there is no snow. Oranges would grow on trees. Houses would have grass lawns and palm trees. Movie stars would walk around so that we would see them in person. "Yea, yea sure", was the reply from unbelieving friends.

Dad decided that he and John Candido were going to drive to California. There were a couple of problems. Neither one could drive and neither one had an automobile.

Dad was forty-nine years old when he applied for a driving license. Applied is used loosely. He talked with one of his American Legion veteran friends who tested drivers. By paying the appropriate licensing fee, he received his driver's license. It was a favor among friends. There was no need to take a driving test; however, the task now became learning to drive an automobile. Two people could teach him. One was his younger brother Dominic and the other was son Lou.

Dad had driven an auto in the early 1920's a few years after being discharged from the service. He and several friends drove a Model T to Southington mountain. There they would practice driving up and down a hill. Why it was called Southington mountain is hard to fathom but it was a steep enough hill for practice. As he drove down the hill, he recalled to us on an occasion when family stories were shared, that he was holding a steering wheel which had without warning become unattached to the steering column. So he and his friends hollered and prayed for divine intervention as they careened down at what was a breakneck or for that matter a deadly speed. The automobile came to rest at the bottom of the hill after coasting for several hundred feet. They had feared putting on the brakes expecting it to veer right or left and so they waited for that divine intervention in the form of gravity to take over. Fortunately, it did.

Now he was faced with the trauma of long ago. He had to drive an automobile for the first time in twenty-plus years. He decided that brother Lou would be the best instructor. On an August Saturday night, he enlisted Lou with Junior and me in the back seat.

He had purchased a 1936 Nash Lafayette sedan. Lou, who had earned a license by practicing with friends, drove the car along Division Street to Long Hill Road to Wolcott Road. There Lou decided that the situation was acceptable for a test run with a new driver. Traffic was nearly empty in this gasoline saving society. Dad took over. The auto lurched once, twice, three times as he let out the clutch. Slowly it began to move forward a little more gently. We drove. He was feeling satisfied. We reached a point where turning back was necessary. Dad decided that a U-turn was appropriate. The turn was attempted without notice to anyone including the few cars on the road. It was also attempted in the middle of a hill. The car could not make the turn. Fortunately with Lou's help and advise which went something like this, "Slam on the brakes! Slam on the brakes!" The car came to a halt against a white barrier below which was a drop of about thirty feet. Driver training did not have an auspicious beginning. The worst however was over. Dad drove a few more times convinced that he could make the journey to California the coming January, 1945 in the Lafayette. After all, he was a man who was quite confident of his ability.

January 31, 1945 arrived and all plans were in place. Dad said his good-byes to each of us. With Junior and me the good-bye was said together. The theme he spoke to us was repeated several times in his subsequent postcards and letters over the next eight months. "Junior,

Paulie, I expect that you will do your best. You must be much better behaved. Lou is gone and you two are the only young men in the home. Can I count on you? Will you do this for me? I won't be here. It's up to you".

Dad and John Candido started out in a snow storm. As he wrote later on, it snowed from Waterbury until they reached Tennessee. The route to avoid the snow was through Connecticut, New York, Pennsylvania, West Virginia, and then into Kentucky. John decided that he could not drive so Dad took on the chore of driving alone. Five months of having a license and now driving sleek highways in the snow was a lesson in learning by immersion. In ten days, they arrived in Los Angeles.

Letters and penny postcards, addressed separately to each of us, began to arrive on a regular basis - two to three times a week - as he drove across country.

The postcards that came to me included:

From Lexington, Kentucky on February 2, 1945, he wrote on a postcard that had in color a picture of General Robert E. Lee on Traveler, "Do you know this fellow, Paul? Are you doing your part without being hollered at?"

Love, Pop

In a postcard dated February 4, 1945 from Fayetteville, Kentucky showing the local post office, he wrote, "In my next letter I will give you all a lecture on Cumberland Mtns., Swanee University - right on top. I told mother about Mt. Carver. This was the worse driving. It must be beautiful in summer".

Dad

On February 6, 1945, postmarked from Ranger, Texas, came a picture of the Texas & Pacific Passenger Station at Fort Worth and the message "How are you behaving boy. Hope I will not be disappointed in you."

Love from Dad

In a postcard of February 9, 1945 that had on the front a picture in color of a young man and woman sitting arm and arm looking over a beautiful valley, he wrote. "Hello Paul, Read this one to Jr." The postcard included a notation in print: Taken from an original oil painting by the noted cowboy artist and poet, L. H. "Dude" Larsen.

Love, Dad

The poem was titled "Dreaming"

Dreaming, dreaming, dreaming
    Of a home that is to be,
Up there in the valley
    In that pretty spot you see.
You can have the crowded cities,
    With their modernistic touch.
Just give us the land of freedom,
    We don't care for near so much.
Just a home there in the valley
    On the banks of that silver stream,
We will go through life together
    Making hardships just a dream.

The poem seemed to represent the hope to be realized in California. A second opportunity to raise a family as was once the dream of Mill Plain.

On February 8, 1945 came a postcard from Big Springs, Texas. The card included a caption "When cornered this species may leap over a cow pony or car and speed to safety. Like the bison herds, now almost extinct." The picture on the card was titled, "Leather and fur for a new pair of chaps" and showed a man with a knife cutting open a jackrabbit that stretched from a tree and was well over ten feet long. It seemed a bit ironic that on one side of the card a statement related the possibility of the extinction of the jackrabbit and on the other side there was a picture of the demise of one such creature being skinned for "leather and fur for a new pair of chaps".

In my files is a postcard sent not to me but to Mom from Dad. On the card is a phrase "Te Adoro" with flowers, hearts, and the holding hands of a man and a woman. On the message side of the card is the day Sat. 2:50 p.m.

Hello Al,

Accept my sincere thoughts from Los Angeles. This card I purchased in the Mexican Village here not far from where I am staying "Te adoro" if you will translate means I adore you. I miss you gal, also all of my family. I went to the PO just 10 minutes ago. No mail. I am going back again before it closes at 5 p.m.

Hoping this will find you all in the Best of Health. Get your sleep and rest.

Love, your husband, Angelo.

In June, 1945, I said good-by to the students in the sixth grade class at Walsh Grammar School. I would miss them I said since they had been my classmates these past several years. For me, it was a touch of sadness mixed with anticipation. My teacher gave me an envelope with my 6th Grade Report Card from Walsh Grammar School June 1945. She said that I should take it with me when I enroll in my new school.

My 6th Grade Report Card from Walsh Grammar School June 1945:

Reading	B
Spelling	A
Arithmetic	A
History	A
Geography	A
Science	A
Language	C
Handwriting	B

Before he left for California, Dad had arranged for Dominic Del Donna to give Junior and me free haircuts while he was gone. Twice a month we would walk to the barber shop just off Bank Street and have our hair cuts. On one such Saturday, while at the shop, there was a Waterbury paper that carried the story of Mussolini's assassination with a picture of Mussolini hanging from a pole upside down and naked. He had been shot several times by Italians seeking revenge.

In the same paper was an on-going story of Byron Nelson, a golf professional, who was making sports history weekly because of an accumulation of golf victories which eventually reached eleven wins.

The days between February, 1945 and August, 1945 were filled with anticipation and hard-work. Holdovers from Mill Plain were a mahogany dining room set, an upright piano made of walnut, an oak bedroom set, linens, pots and pans, silverware, a china set and china made from milk glass, and all the "saved for retirement" collection stored in the bottom drawers.

Movers needed to be contacted who were willing to transport to California- no small feat during the war years. With reluctance, the piano was sold, then the dining room set, and then the bedroom set. Newspapers were collected and breakables were wrapped and stored for the day the moving company would arrive.

In the last week of July, 1945, as I was want to do, I stuck my foot under the cold water tap so as to be able to put my feet in the hot bath water. Unfortunately, the hot water tap and not the cold water was running. As a result, my skin blistered and my foot swelled to a significant and scary size. I hollered to Mom. Mom hollered to Tessie, "Go next door and ask Mr. Evans if he will take us to emergency." Mr. Evans came and we took off for Waterbury hospital. My foot swelled and the skin pealed off. The doctor applied ointment, gauze, and loaned us a pair of crutches. My fear was whether I could make the trip to California on crutches.

Dad wrote to Mom. I have a house for us and it's time to move. Mom was forty-three years old and was about to head west with four of her five children to meet her husband who was not quite fifty. Her concerns were expressed to her four children. "We are going to be alone together, No one will protect us except ourselves. We need to stay together at all times. You can not be out of my sight." To Lena and Tessie, she entrusted Junior and me for special care. "Lena and Tess, it's up to you as the older ones to especially watch Paulie and Junior. Don't let them wander off or we will never find them. You understand?" Lena and Tess now resigned to California agreed to shepherd us across three thousand miles of travel.

The movers came and packed dishes and china into barrels, which were the only type of container material available during the war years. The barrels were loaded on a truck with assurances that the van would arrive in California within two weeks with the china and glasses unbroken.

On Monday, August 6th, Mom took Junior and me to see my Grandmother Mocciola at a convalescent home. Grandma had suffered from diabetes for many years and a few weeks prior to our visit, she had to have her leg amputated due to the gangrene. It was a tearful good-bye for my mother who idolized her mother. Mom asked us to leave the room after we said our good-byes. We waited on a dirt road in front of the home until she came out. She was weeping softly as we headed for the bus stop. It was the last time we would see Grandma. For some reason, I remember that the road outside the convalescent home was lined with willows.

On Tuesday, August 7, 1945, my bandages came off. Fortunately, my toes and foot looked normal.

Mom called her brother-in- law Albert, (Dad's brother) who lived in New York, and said that we would be arriving on the New York, New Haven, and Hartford Railroad at Grand Central Station on Friday, August 10, 1945 at 9:00 a.m. He was prepared to meet us and to chaperone us to the All American Bus Lines depot.

On Thursday, August 9th, we left 230 Orange Street and headed for 108 Maple Street, Grandfather Mocciola's home, where we spent the night. Mom worried about the bed. "Had it been aired since Grandma went into the hospital?" We survived. On the morning of Friday, August 10, we walked to the Waterbury Railroad Station to board the train. It was our first train ride.

Uncle Albert met us in New York at Grand Central Train Station. He was with a friend and together they put us in a taxi (another first) and we headed for the bus depot.

Within an hour we were on an All-American Bus Line 1930's vintage and heading for Los Angeles. The bus was white with red striping that declared its company's name. The engine was under a hood that stuck out as did all such trucks of such vintage.

We found seats and kept them as a matter of course for the entire bus ride. We sat on the left side of the bus. Junior and I were together. Lena and Tess sat behind us to watch over us. Mom sat in front of us to be sure that she would guard us from the front. The passengers were a varied assortment of travelers. Servicemen were heading home. Most of the other travelers were heading west to be left off at some point along the route. The head driver said that he and his partner would take us as far as St. Louis and then another driving team would take us the rest of the way. He gave us the rules. There would be no stops during the night - so the best thing to do is sleep. Since there were no toilets on the bus, we would have to be patient until we reached a rest stop. There would be a breakfast, lunch, and supper stop. We would have two breaks at about 10:00 a.m. and 2:30 p.m. We were required to be on the bus when it was ready to leave after any stop or be left behind. That warning was sufficient for Mom to turn to us and to admonish us once again to behave, stay together, and don't go off alone.

In one's youth, bladder problems are not an issue fortunately so waiting for stops was not a problem.

We headed for the promised land.

We traveled through the rolling hills and farmlands of Pennsylvania. It was a scene that we had not witnessed before. All we knew was Waterbury with its three story tar-papered covered houses. Neither Lena, Tessie, Junior, nor I had been out of the city into the country. The green rolling hills and the farms were beyond what we had ever experienced. By late afternoon, we arrived in Pittsburgh. Passing through the city, we became aware of a strange sight. The sides of the buildings were covered with a black type of powder. "Mom, why are the buildings so black? "That's soot and it comes from their steel mills. They make steel in Pittsburgh and that's the result". The image was indelibly printed in my mind - tall building covered with soot." "Are their houses covered with soot too?" "I don't' think so - only the buildings close to where they make steel."

Columbus, Ohio was like a story book city. We had rarely seen separate homes since leaving Mill Plain but these were so different and so beautiful to witness. Each home was situated on a lot by itself with lawns, trees, and shrubbery.

As we traveled across the states of Ohio, Indiana, and Illinois, the country was beginning to look much like the songs we sang of "Oh beautiful for spacious skies". We began to experience the descriptions that teachers provided when they talked of their travels. "Children, the United States is a beautiful country with green pastures, rolling farm lands, barns, cattle, corn fields..." It was a magnificent sight to see first hand.

On Saturday, August 11, 1945, we arrived in St. Louis. Our first major shock involving segregation occurred. The bus station had separate toilets labeled "colored and white". Mom was furious chiefly because waiting in line to use the facilities was a burden given the number of travelers. Once the bus passengers used the rest rooms, they had to rush to be on the bus before it left. Mother obeyed the bus driver's rules, and if the bus driver said he would leave without any straggling passengers then he would leave without us. So she decided the best answer was to use the colored toilet which had no waiting line. Going into a colored toilet was not breaking the rules because such an idea of two toilets did not make sense to her. She had not experienced such a thing in Connecticut and separate toilets when there was a need for her children was not acceptable. Thus she sent Junior and me into the white men's toilet since there was no line and she with Lena and Tessie went into the colored women's toilet, much to the dismay of several onlookers.

Providence has a way of rewarding the daring souls who seek greater levels of human dignity, and my mother was rewarded. Upon leaving the rest room, we headed toward the bus as the driver had given his usual five minute warning. As she headed for the bus, Mom looked into her purse for some reason and that is when she went into a panic. Her wallet was missing with her directions, all her cash, and important papers. "Hold the bus she called to the driver. My wallet is missing." She ran to the traveler's aid desk and told them her story. We followed quickly behind expecting to be stranded in Missouri without money for food or shelter or for that matter a bus ride to Los Angeles. From the time she had headed from the rest room toward the bus and discovered that the wallet was missing was possibly ten minutes. The traveler's aid smiled and said tell me your name which my mother did. Then came providence. The woman said, "that colored man over there", and she pointed, "said he found your wallet on the floor near the bathroom. He returned it. just a minute ago." My mother looked into the wallet. Everything was in order. She ran to the man. "Thank you! Thank you! Please, let me give you some money as a reward" "No ma'am. Thank you but no. You traveling with your family?", and he looked at us, "Well, good luck to you and have a good trip." That was it. He walked off. We got on the bus.

We arrived in Oklahoma City after a sixteen hour ride. The landscape had changed from green meadow lands to a slightly rolling country side. From there, we headed to Texas. It was apparent why Texans bragged about the size of their state. For two and one half days we rode that bus through Texas. Endless hours faced us of flat open territory with only a few houses or small towns in between the hours of travel. Dallas/Fort Worth came and went and then we passed through Pecos and then finally we headed toward El Paso and the end of the Texas trail. When we passed through the western part of Texas, we saw people walking along the roads and working the fields as we came to some cultivated area. Most of them seemed to be darker in complexion. They were brown or olive skinned - much like Italians. When we asked other travelers, we were told that they were Mexicans from Mexico or they were Mexican-Americans who lived in this part of the country.

We passed through El Paso on Sunday evening at about sundown. The streets of the city teemed with Mexicans. Many dressed in blue pants made of a canvas-like cloth. It was a pant style that we had not seen before. Their hats were not cowboy types but were more rounded and brimmed. Their belts were wide with wide buckles. They generally wore bandannas around their necks. Their shirts were white and shiny as if made of silk.

It was also in Texas that a sign advertising a soft drink began to appear that we did not have in Waterbury. It wasn't Coca Cola, or Pepsi-Cola, or Seven-Up but Dr. Pepper. The signs read that we should drink Dr. Pepper at 10:00, 2:00 and 4:00 o'clock. A passenger told Mom that it was healthy because it was made with prune juice.

From El Paso we passed through Las Cruces and then to Tucson. On Tuesday, August 14, 1945, we arrived in Phoenix and stopped at a cafe on the main street of the town. The temperature was 118 degrees at 5:00 p.m.. The town, dusty with sand from the desert, was small and relatively easy to bus through. The center of the town apparently consisted chiefly of this main highway with its stores for those persons who were traveling. At the cafe, Mom let me order hot apple pie topped with melted cheese. That order was a mistake. Whether it was the heat or the hot apple pie or the melted cheese, I am not sure. Fortunately, the bus had bags to use for throwing up and that is what I did for the next hour or so. It was outside Phoenix that I swore off hot apple pie and melted cheese for life.

At times in one's life, there are moments that are vividly remembered. The scene is called up and viewed in one's mind as if it was occurring all over again. Thus it was with the next several hours of my life.

As we left Phoenix and headed on the last leg of the journey, it was about five o'clock in the afternoon of August 14, 1945. As a few hours went by, we began to pass through small towns. As we passed, sirens were sounding. Whistles could be heard toward the town's centers. After the first town and realizing the same sounds were occurring in the next town and the next, it became apparent that something of importance was occurring. "It's got to be the end of the war." Hopes began to rise. "It's got to be. What else can it be?" Just before the bus crossed into California, the driver stopped at a small store in Yuma where we heard the news officially. The Japanese had surrendered, and the war was over. It was a celebration as we crossed the border into California at about 1:00 a.m. in the morning of August 15, 1945. It was as if we were a first - the first to cross into California after the end of the war. By 6:00 a.m. we arrived at the San Diego bus station. Throughout the station were servicemen -mostly sailors- sleeping on benches, the floor, counters wherever. "It was quite a celebration", the station attendant offered, "Most of them just settled down a few hours ago."

At 9:30 a.m. we arrived in Los Angeles at the bus station on 6th and Los Angeles Street.

Dad was waiting. He ran to the bus and hugged Mom and then each of us. Junior and I were happy; he was really pleased to see us. We walked the streets of Los Angeles. Cocktail bars, taverns, and stores were decorated with flags and many resembled an air raid shelter with sand bags piled in front. We walked past Clifton's cafeteria. We looked up every chance we could because we saw palm tree after palm tree. We had arrived in Paradise.

Paradise was 2117 West 74th Street. Dad had purchased a house for $6,500 and furnished it with whatever was available from Sears Roebuck. Maybe it was the climate or maybe our age, but the skirmishes between Junior (now wanting to be called Angelo) and me ended. Junior and I found a new way of dealing with each other and thus strife for my mother and my father was over. Peace and tranquillity prevailed. Dad never had to admonish or discipline us again.

Bold beginnings have a way of reinforcing themselves. For Mom and Dad, it was a daring choice to start again 3,000 miles away from family and friends. The promise of a good life in California was an act of courage that could manifest itself potentially into new opportunities in the country that they loved.

Epilogue

On September 1, 1945, the barrels of china and glassware arrived. When she opened the barrels, Mom began to cry. A significant number of pieces were broken.

The next day however the arrival of a telegram made the broken items insignificant. For on September 2, 1945, a telegram arrived.

Dad,

Arrived in States. Safe and sound. See you soon.

Love,

Lou

Lou came home, enrolled in Loyola University under the GI Bill, and graduated.

After the American Civil War, America was challenged by the loss of hundreds of thousands of men from both the North and the South who would never return home. They would never write the plays, the songs, or the books. These men would never invent or build or contribute in the future of the country. The Civil War veterans who did come home faced an uncertain future. For many it was the frontier that saved them. To offset the loss from the Civil War casualties of this intellect and skill, America replenished its human intellect and brawn through immigration. Thus, the United States survived and grew stronger.

After World War II, there were no frontiers for returning servicemen and women.

The generation that grew up in the 1930's and 1940's and overcame a depression and fought a war has been called America's greatest generation. Such an accolade may be worthy of the achievements of these men and women.

The Congress of the United States enacted one of the finest laws in our history when it passed the GI Bill of Rights. That legislation made it possible for so many of those men and women to continue to contribute to the American society because of the opportunities it afforded through a college education or through trade school training.

These college graduates became the teachers, authors, lawyers, police and fire fighters, doctors, ministers of the 1950's and beyond.

Those veterans that attended trade schools, opened their own businesses and also became the backbone of the economic system.

The immigration of the 1870's to the early 1900's may have been a fortunate happenstance. The solution of the GI Bill was enlightened leadership and legislation.

Angelo Possmato- World War I, Age 24, 1919

Angelo Possmato- Age 21, 1916 (below)

Angelo Possmato- upper right, Age 21, 1916

Albina Mocciola- on left, Age 16, 1917

Waterbury Clock Shop, Albina Mocciola, bottom right, Age 14, 1915

Angelo Possmato- Baseball on Sunday, Age 20, bottom right

Angelo (middle), Age 27, with barber friends

**Monsignor valdambrini receiving an award from veterans.
Angelo Possemato on far right.**

Angelo Possmato, Age 24, 1919, on right

A barbers' union supporter

Albina Mocciola, Age 17, 1918

Mill Plain- 350 Atwood Avenue, Blizzard of 1938

Mill Plain- Louis and Lena with Tess in carriage

Mill Plain- Junior and Paul, Savan Rock, Circa 1936

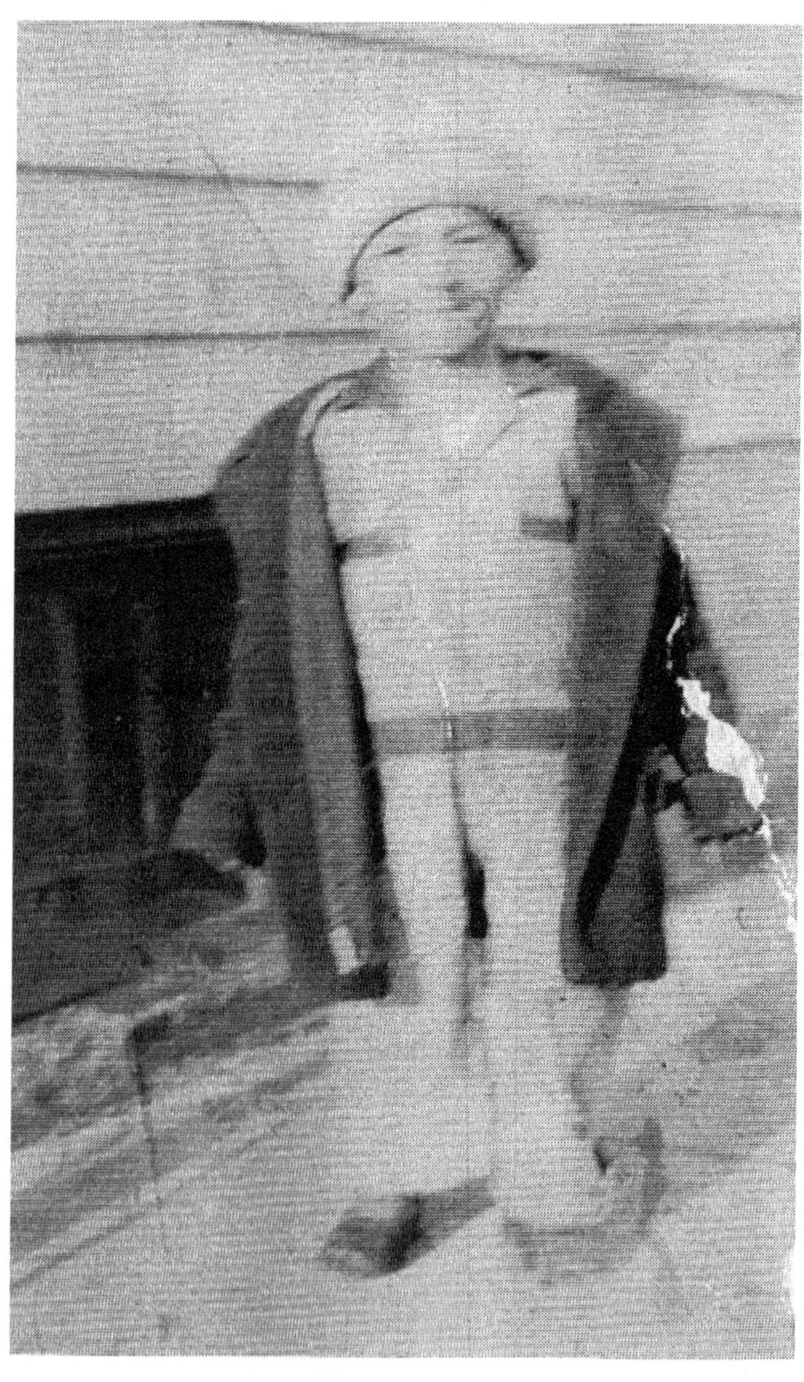

Mill Plain- Junior, Age 4, 1935

Orange Street, 1944- Mickie, Mom, and Tess

Orange Street, 1944-Mickie, Lou, Paul, and Junior

Orange Street, 1944-Tess and Mickie

About the Author

Paul Possemato was born in Waterbury, Connecticut in 1933. He and his family moved to Los Angeles, California in 1945. He has bachelor's degree in Political Science from UCLA and a master's and a doctorate from the University of Southern California.

He has been a teacher, high school principal, and a superintendent of schools in the southern California area. His honors include UCLA Educator of the Year and California Administrator of the Year district/county category. His background as a writer of professional materials led him to record events that influenced him and his family during the depression and war years.

He has been married to Peggy since 1960 and they have one daughter, Carla.